Michael's
THE NEW GUIDE

FLORENCE

THE NEW GUIDE

Michael's

FLORENCE

Managing Editor
Michael Shichor

Series Editor
Amir Shichor

INBAL TRAVEL INFORMATION LTD.

Inbal Travel Information Ltd.
P.O.Box 1870 Ramat Gan 52117
Israel

Intl. ISBN 965-288-127-9

Text: Dov Ancona
Graphic design: Michel Opatowski
Cover design: Bill Stone
Photography: Yossi Shrem, Geremy Feldman
Photo editor: Sharon Bentov
Editorial: Sharona Johan, Yitzhak Shichor
D.T.P.: Michael Michelson
Maps: Michael Michelson, Itzik Hazan
Printed by Havatzelet Press Ltd.

**Sales in the UK
and Europe:**
Kuperard (London) Ltd.
32-34 Gordon House Road
London NW5 1LP

**Distribution in the UK
and Europe:**
Bailey Distribution Ltd.
Learoyd Road
New Romney
Kent TN28 8X

U.K. ISBN 1-85733-123-0

CONTENTS

INTRODUCTION

FLORENCE

TABLE OF MAPS

Preface

Florence, the capital of Tuscany, is a cultural feast. Home of such masters as Michelangelo, Leonardo da Vinci, Dante and Machiavelli, this city has contributed to the world invaluable artistic and intellectual treasures.

Florence's museums and galleries house some of the world's most glorious masterpieces of Renaissance art, including Michelangelo's *David* and Leonardo's *Annunciation*. The grand palaces, magnificent churches and impressive sculptures adorning its streets and squares make a visit here unforgettable.

Framing Florence is a green belt of rolling hills, villas and parks. A day or two in the environs of Florence – Siena, San Gimignano, Arezzo, Empoli, Pisa and other charming places – will round out your Florentine experience.

Our writer, Dov Ancona, assisted by the staff of Inbal Travel Information, spent months researching and collecting the information found in these pages, to bring you the best of this wonderful city in the most effective and enjoyable way.

By directing you to the city's highlights and by helping you sense its pulse, we hope to make your visit to Florence a most memorable one. We trust that you'll find Florence as captivating as we do.

Michael Shichor

Using this Guide

In order to reap maximum benefit from the information in this guide, we advise the traveler to carefully read the following passage. The facts contained in this book were compiled to help the tourist find his or her way around and to ensure that he enjoys his stay to the upmost.

The "Introduction" provides details which will help you make the early decisions and arrangements for your trip. We suggest that you carefully review the material, so that you will be more organized and set for your visit. Upon arrival in Florence, you will feel familiar and comfortable with the city.

The tour routes, laid out geographically, lead the visitor up and down the city's streets, providing a survey of the sites and calling attention to all those details which deepen one's familiarity with Florence, and make a visit there so much more enjoyable.

The reader will notice that certain facts tend to recur. This is deliberate; it enables the tourist who starts out from a point other than the one we choose to be no less informed. The result is a flexibility in personal planning.

Following the tour routes, we have included a selection of excursions, which are all extremely interesting. Each of these excursions makes for a very pleasant trip out of the city.

The rich collection of maps covers the tour routes and special attractions in great detail. Especially prepared for this book, they will certainly add to the efficiency and pleasure of your exploration of Florence.

A concise list of "Musts" follows, describing those sites without which your visit is not complete.

Since Florence is highly esteemed for its cuisine and shopping, a special chapter is devoted to "Making the Most of Your Stay" in the city. Here you will find a broad range of possibilities to suit your budget, needs and tastes.

As most tourists arriving in Florence are not familiar with the Italian language, we have added a short dictionary containing some basic words; these may help you while traveling.

To further facilitate the use of this guide, we have included a detailed index. It includes all the major sites mentioned throughout the book. Consult the index to find something by name and it will refer you to the place where it is mentioned in greatest detail.

During your visit you will have many fascinating experiences. We have therefore left several blank pages at the end of the guide. These are for you to jot down your observations, thoughts, and reactions along the way.

Because times and cities are dynamic, an important rule of thumb when traveling should be to consult local sources of information. Tourists are liable to encounter certain inaccuracies in this guide, and for this, we apologize.

In this guide we have tried to present updated information in a way which allows for an easy, safe and economical visit. For this purpose, we have included a short questionnaire and will be most grateful for those who will take the time to complete it and send it to us.

Have a pleasant and exciting trip – Bon Voyage!

PART ONE – AN OVERVIEW

Florence, the birth-place of the Renaissance, of the Italian language and of modern banking was for centuries a leading power, having achieved its greatness without great wars of conquest, without the use of force and without mass indoctrination of the millions.

In every street and alley of Florence, you can almost feel the glorious past, so well preserved. In a way, to paraphrase Churchill, it can be said about Florence that so few gave so much and for so long to so many: not only in the fields of art, science, economics and culture in general, but also in *Joie de Vivre*, in creativity, in vision.

History

The first settlement of what was at the time a not very reliable ford of the River Arno probably dates from the Iron Age. More than twenty five centuries ago, the ford was also used by the Etruscans, who decided to build their own district higher up above the valley, on the top of a neighbouring hill, far from the frequent outbursts of the Arno.

Rome, the greatest road building civilization of ancient times, embarked in the 2nd century BC on the laying of the northward bound Via Cassia; just about at the point where the Roman road crossed the Arno today stands the historic Ponte Vecchio of Florence. Thus Florence was born, around the ford. Its Latin name, *Florentia*, meant "due to prosper". Prosper it did under Roman rule, if only briefly. Built around a segment of the Via Cassia and the river ford, it became a walled fortress, like most Roman outposts. The segment of the Roman road was soon substituted by a wooden bridge, the first to be built.

The town had four gates, and beyond the walls the Romans built, as was their custom, an amphitheatre, a river pier, an aqueduct and baths.

INTRODUCTION

Ponte Vecchio – "The Ancient Bridge"

In 285AD, Florence also became the seat of Rome's regional administrator, the *Corrector*. With the fall of the Roman Empire in 476, the Via Cassia became utterly insecure and practically deserted, and Florence virtually disappeared from the annals of history for several centuries. As was true of most Italian cities in the early Middle Ages, Florence was frequently invaded and captured by different nations: the Byzantines (541), the Huns (550), the Lombards (580) and later several Holy Roman Emperors. In 801, Charlemagne took over the town, and began its restoration.

The 11th century brought with it a long series of adventures: the Crusades, the long drawn contest between the Church and the Holy Roman Empire, the struggle for supremacy among princes and dukes.

Florence won its independence in 1115, in the shadow of the great papal-imperial wars. Having no great imperialistic ambitions, Florence simply had to ensure its immediate safety. The little town of Fiesole, positioned close by and uncomfortably high above Florence's plain, often posed a daily threat; in 1125 it was razed to the ground by the Florentines, except for its Cathedral.

Figline (32km southeast of Florence) and Empoli (32km west of Florence) were Florence's next conquests. More caution was exercised in dealing with more powerful neighbours like Arezzo, Pistoia, Pisa, Siena and Lucca. Florence began to develop as an industrial and mercantile power. The first *arti* (forerunners of guilds and corporations) emerged toward the end of the 12th century.

Florence's wool and silk industries became the main suppliers of high quality cloth to all European courts. Florence's architects and builders were on demand not only at home (the Baptistry and the Church of San Miniato date from this period), but also in all the richer towns in the region. These enterprises brought in a great flow of income in gold and jewels, and a handful of sharp-minded, enterprising families set themselves up in business as the bankers of Europe.

With the onset of the Crusades, Florence became one of the main suppliers to the great passing armies. When no cash was available, Florentine merchants sold on credit, which meant power and economic growth. They set up new *arti* and *corporazioni* and issued what soon became the major European currency, the *florin* (short for "florentin", of course). This 23 karat gold coin was traded in all the major money markets of Europe in a matter of few months.

In order to protect its newly-acquired assets, Florence begin to give thought to war. In 1173 it joined the papal alliance that defeated Frederick the Redbeard.

The 13th century was a time of local strife in Italy between two conflicting factions: the *Guelfi*, who supported the Pope, and the *Ghibellini*, standard bearers of the Empire. Hoping to resolve at least some of these political conflicts, Florence set itself up as a *Signoria*. This was a new term, invented by Florence to make the idea of absolute rule by a reigning prince more palatable to the masses.

In 1262 the Florentines invented the *letter of exchange* (a precursor of modern "futures" trading), which became the major tool of international banking. Letters of exchange, gold, jewels and other items of worth began flowing from the main centres of Europe to the vaults of those few great Florentine families. Thus were born Europe's first banks.

The Florentines next turned to architecture, creating the harmoniously expressive Romanesque style (introduced by Arnolfo di Cambio) which so brilliantly exploited the

pastel-tinted marbles of the Tuscan hillsides.

At the same time Cimabue's and Giotto's school of figurative art finally abandoned the structures of the Byzantine era for a freer, more spontaneously sensual and vivacious style.

Toward the end of the 13th century, Florence's bankers had enough power to abolish the rule of the *Signoria*, which they replaced with a republican structure, administered by the upper class of merchants, in alliance with the stronger *corporazioni*.

The new rulers again found themselves bitterly divided into two hostile factions, the popist *Guelfi* and their *Ghibellini* adversaries. Almost as soon as the *Guelfi* succeeded in ousting their *Ghibellini* rivals, a new source of strife split the victors into two new enemy factions known as the *Bianchi* and the *Neri* (Whites and Backs).

Florence had become one of Italy's major political powers, together with Venice, Milan, Genoa and the Papal State. Moreover, Florence became the bubbling cauldron of new, creative modes of written expression, with Dante, Petrarch and Boccaccio abandoning the traditional literary Latin for the effervescent *Dolce Stil Nuovo* (Sweet New Style). With new life breathed into the *Lingua Volgare* (the commoners' Florentine vernacular), it soon became the recognized language of Italy.

However, Florence's days as a self-governed "republic" were numbered. Whenever one of the great families threatened the city's delicate balance of power, its rivals sought to put it down. The Buondelmontis, the Fifantis, the Ubertis, the Acciaioli, the Bonaccorsis, the Pazzis and the Medicis plotted and fought each other for more than a century, blocking the growth of Florence's military power.

When forced to engage in war, Florence used its economic power to buy the services of the best captains of fortune. Thus, even war became a very costly affair.

The most severe crisis of the epoch peaked in 1348, with the outbreak of a terrible plague. Within a few weeks, the population of Florence was halved, going from little less than 100,000 people to 45,000. This catastrophe had been preceded by a grave financial debacle. The British Crown, its coffers depleted by centuries of wars and deeply indebted to several great Florentine families, became insolvent. In only a few years, four major Floren-

tine banking families were forced to close their London doors. At the same time, several years of drought brought the lower classes of Florence to the edge of starvation.

While citizens of Siena, Pisa, Leghorn and other cities sank into apathy and despair because of the plague, the Florentine spirit proved its invincibility: as soon as the illness abated, the city opened its gates to any farmer wishing to settle in town. Severe regulations that limited the rights of non-Florentines were eliminated, and in the course of less than a decade Florence was again on its feet.

This was the time of the harshest class wars Florence had ever known. Two new powers emerged besides the aristocracy and the great merchant families: the *popolo grasso* (literally, the "fat people"), leaders of the 7 major *arti* (guilds) – and the *popolo minuto* (the "negligible people"), of the actual workers in those and in the other 14 minor *arti*.

Both those groups had a hand in city politics during the second half of the 14th century: the *popolo grasso* ruled the city for more than two decades; the *popolo minuto* led a rebellion in 1378 (called "La Revolta de' Ciompi"), which ended, however, with the triumph of their *popolo grasso* bosses.

At the beginning of the 15th century the Medicis, a merchant family that had already established itself as the greatest banker of Florence and of all Europe, were ousted and exiled by a coalition of old families, headed

One of the Medicis' villas

by the super rich Strozzis and by the overwhelmingly powerful Albizzis. The Medicis were forced to seek shelter in Padua.

In 1434 Cosimo the Elder (*il Vecchio*), head of the Medicis, returned from exile, massacred the Pazzis, exiled the Albizzis and set up court in Florence, not only as a conqueror, but also as the protector of the arts and letters. Among his protegés were the great architect and sculptor Brunelleschi and most of the great painters of those times, like the Lippi brothers and Donatello.

Cosimo il Vecchio died in 1464, and was succeeded briefly by his son Piero, whose precarious health left him little time to test in action his political and business acumen. He died in 1469, leaving the new Medici *Signoria* to his two sons, Lorenzo and Giuliano.

Giuliano, little more than a glorified playboy, was killed when the Pazzis made a last attempt to avenge themselves, hoping to oust the Medicis from power; Lorenzo was wounded. In the end, the Pazzis failed and Lorenzo became Florence's only ruler.

Lorenzo is considered the father of the Renaissance (and also of Pope Leon X); he was the protector of Leonardo da Vinci and of Michelangelo, of Botticelli and Ghirlandaio, of Verrocchio, Brunelleschi and Pollaiolo. Under Lorenzo the

Magnificent *(il Magnifico)* the Medicis reached their peak of glory and power.

But this peak didn't last. Florence's and the Medicis' finances went from bad to worse. Even the great Medici Bank failed, first in London and then in Bruges. In Florence itself, the Medicis bank was forced to close its doors two years after Lorenzo's death, in 1494.

The sudden financial crisis caused an uprising, forcing Lorenzo's son, Piero, to flee, leaving the town in anarchy. Florence fell prey to the charisma of Girolamo Savonarola, a Dominican monk and naïve social reformer whose followers looted palaces and burned furniture and art works for almost four years.

Savonarola was excommunicated by Pope Alexander VI

(who also belonged to the Medici family) and condemned to die by fire for herecy; Savonarola was executed in May 1498 on Piazza della Signoria. After several years of chaos, the Medicis were able to make a triumphal comeback in 1512, under the sponsorship of the King of Spain.

The next Medici rulers did not distinguish themselves in government; the real power had in essence passed onto the hands of the so-called Medici Popes: Leon X (1513-1521), Lorenzo's son and Clemente VII (1523-1534), Giuliano's son.

The Medicis ruled Florence (and most of Tuscany with it) for the next two centuries, until 1737. During those two centuries Florence lost most of its political power, but it never lost its cultural primacy in Italy and Europe, and the city continued to grow.

Giorgio Vasari, Bartolomeo Ammannati and Bernardo Buontalenti, three great architects, restored and rebuilt Palazzo Pitti into a royal residence. Buontalenti also built the great fortress of San Giorgio (or the Belvedere). Across town, another new fort, San Giovanni (or *Forte da Basso*) helped to enclose the whole city under the Medicis' wings. In 1570 Buontalenti also completed the restructuring of a network of ill-reputed alleys into what became Florence's ghetto, where the Jewish community was forcedly enclosed.

The Medicis' successors, the Lorena Grand Dukes, ruled for little more than a century, dedicating most of their efforts to the economic and agricultural development of Tuscany; the interests and the arts of their capital were at times neglected.

In 1865 Florence briefly became the capital of the nascent kingdom of Italy; a new wave of building and renewal resulted in the razing of most of the old walls and in the paving of a net of wide and pleasant avenues. Most of the great old monuments were transformed into museums, and the unique artistic heritage of Florence was protected from being sold or looted away.

Florence did not suffer greatly in the two great wars of the 20th century; however, in World War II the retreating Nazi army bombed and

destroyed some of the buildings and all of the bridges in Florence, except the historic Ponte Vecchio.

Nature has repeatedly threatened the heritage of Florence: the most grievous damages were caused by the great flood of 1966, when the Arno rose to unheard of levels, invading the lower sections of town to a height of more than 5m. Thousands of volunteers from Italy and from several other countries laboured for months to clean up the streets and the great halls of Florence, but many works of art were damaged beyond repair.

A Brief Chronology

10th century BC– First prehistoric settlements around the Arno River ford.

2nd century BC – Rome establishes a military camp near the ford. The Romans build the Via Cassia and a wooden bridge across the Arno.

285 – Emperor Diocletianus makes Florence capital of the district.

541 – A Byzantine army occupies Florence.

550 – The Hun chieftain Totila loots the town and sets fire to it.

580 – The Lombards occupy Florence.

801 – Emperor Charlemagne enters Florence and begins reconstruction work.

1078 – The great Countess Matilde di Canossa builds her castle (Castello di Altafronte) in Florence.

1115 – On Countess Matilde's death, Florence becomes an independent city.

1125 – Florence conquers and destroys Fiesole.

1138 – Florence is ruled by *consuls* .

1179 – The Uberti family ousts the consuls.

1182 – The first *arte* (the wool workers guild) is established.

1207 – After years of strife, the rule of the town is assigned to a foreign-born *podestà* (appointed mayor); the first is Gualfredotto from Milan.

1262 – Florentine bankers issue the *lettere di cambio*, predecessor of today's cheque.

1293 – The *arti* of merchants and craftsmen overthrow the ancient aristocracy.

1348 – The great plague spreads throughout Florence.

1406 – Florence defeats and annexes Pisa.

1421 – Florence acquires and rules Leghorn.

1434 – Cosimo the Elder returns to Florence and founds the new *Signoria* .

1464 – Death of Cosimo *Il Vecchio*.

1469-1492 – The golden era of Lorenzo *the Magnificent* de' Medici.

1494-1498 – Girolamo Savonarola institutes a reformation.

1498-1503 – The first of the "Minor Medicis", Piero II.
1503-1519 – Lorenzo II rules.
1519-1537 – Alessandro rules and is murdered by his cousin
        Lorenzino.
1569-1574 – Cosimo I de Medici becomes Granduke of Tuscany.
1574-1609 – Ferdinando I becomes Granduke of Tuscany.
1609-1621 – Cosimo II rules.
1621-1670 – Ferdinando II rules.
1670-1701 – Cosimo III rules.
1701-1737 – Gian Gastone, the last of the Medicis.
1737-1859 – The Granduchy of Tuscany passes to the House of
        Lorraine.
1865-1871 – Florence is made the capital of Italy.
1916-1960 – Florence resumes its role in culture as Italy's leading
        city.
1966 – A great flood damages a large part of Florence's artistic
        heritage.

The Shape of Florence

The streets that formed the original Roman town are easily picked out because of their net-like plan. The Roman perimeter encloses the Duomo at the north-eastern corner, the Palazzo Vecchio at the south-eastern corner, Piazza Trinita near the river and the Chiesa di Santa Maria Novella at the north-western end.

Later Florence grew, gradually incorporating old farmland and hamlets, until in the Middle Ages it occupied the whole area circumscribed by the river and the great ring arteries of today: Viale Rosselli, Viale Belfiore, Via Strozzi, Viale Spartaco Lavagnini, Viale Matteotti, Viale Gramsci and Viale Amendola.

Across the river there were already at least three bridges, which joined the old city to the "new" *Oltrarno* ("beyond the Arno") neighbourhoods. It was only several centuries later that Florence expanded to the hilly grounds north and south of the river, with their less monumental yet uncommonly attractive quarters.

Topographically, classic Florence remains to this day a rather flat rectangular space in which the majority of historic and artistic highlights are found. The perimeter of this rectangle runs from the Santa Maria Novella Railway Station, to St. Mark's Museum, to the Church of Santa Croce and the National Library beside it on the river, to Palazzo Pitti and Santa Maria del Carmine on the Oltrarno and back north to the railway station.

Beyond this rectangle there are some of Florence's most

pleasant grounds and park-lands, where there is much to be seen; the Cascine park and Hippodrome along the northern bank of the Arno; the Stibbert Museum and San Marco Vecchio on the northern heights; and beyond – the Oltrarno, S. Miniato, S. Salvatore, the Belvedere Fortress, Poggio Imperiale and Bellosguardo.

Florence owes much of its charm to the quality of its environs. The reddish soil of Tuscany, the vineyards and olive groves that almost reach the city's suburbs, the luxuriant parks and gardens of its many great villas, create an atmosphere of pastoral relaxation. At the same time, the city itself rises upon flat country, dangerously exposed to the moods of its river, the capricious Arno. The architects of Florence were forced to use their creativity in order to erect a city of great charm and beauty on such undependable natural foundations.

Climate

Situated relatively far from the sea, in a sheltered plain under

A panoramic vista of Florence

the shadow of the Appennini mountains, Florence enjoys moderate winters, glorious autumns and springs; high summer in Florence may be torrid, with temperature well above the 30°C and with a high humidity quotient.

Florence's Art Legacy

Painting and sculpture, architecture and music, poetry and prose, science and fantasy – Florence has it all.

While captains and princes in Italy and in most of Europe were busy designing plots and counter plots in an endless struggle for power and territories, the Florentines strove to seek joy of living, profit, handicraft and creativity.

The year 1115 is the natural date for the beginning of this great saga of the arts, the year in which Florence began its independent political life as a free comune. In those days – of endless wars between the Empire and the Papacy, of the great Crusades, of the emergence of many of Europe's

princely courts – the arts were still strongly influenced by the Aristotelian doctrine as it had been transplanted and transmuted by the Church Fathers.

Florence had all the basic ingredients required for a breakthrough of new ideas, new forms, new contents and new goals. It was a deeply religious city; it was not powerful enough to represent a real threat to Emperors or Popes; and it aspired to get ever richer, to better itself and to compete with its neighbours.

In the Middle Ages the arts were strictly connected with religion. Architects, painters and sculptors abstained not only from lay subjects, but also from any expression of worldliness. Architects built mostly churches and chapels. From that epoch we have hundreds of portrayals of the Madonna, of Christ, and of New Testament scenes in which the human figure is carefully idealised and stylised, void of human emotions.

Florence's art life peaked after the 17th century. While Europe went into two centuries of baroque and rococo architecture, sculpture and painting, the Capital of the Renaissance renounced its leadership. Perhaps it had reached perfection and knew that further efforts would have necessarily been an anticlimax. Maybe it was a normal fact of life: art follows success; and Florence's power and wealth were definitely on the ebb. Altogether, this sad twilight of the arts may have been to our great good fortune: to it we owe the hub of Florence as we see it today, in all its harmonious, proud Renaissance glory.

Monumental art at the Palazzo Vecchio

Architecture

The first signs of a new era were evident in Florence already by the middle of the 12th century. The Baptistry, San Miniato, the Santi Apostoli and several great mansions had inaugurated the splendid Florentine Romanesque style, with its horizontal stresses, open arches and pastel-coloured marble decorations.

This architectural approach strongly indicated a return to man's earthly life, as opposed to the ascetics of the vertical lines and the static images in Byzantine art. Not less innovative was the Florentine Gothic style, reflected in the structures of Santa Maria Novella, Santa Croce, Santa Trinita, Orsanmichele, the Duomo, the Campanile, the Signoria Lodge and Palace and the Podestà Palace.

We owe most of medieval Florence to one of its foremost architects of the Renaissance, Arnolfo di Cambio; his work includes the Cathedral, the Basilica di Santa Croce, Palazzo Ferroni and the Church of Orsanmichele (the name is short for Orto San Michele – St. Michael's Garden).

The Renaissance blossomed fully in the 15th century, under the rule of the first Medicis, mainly Cosimo il Vecchio and Lorenzo il Magnifico. Florence's glory and wealth found suitable expression in the unequalled creations of several great architects:

Two of Florence's most distinguished structures – the Duomo and the tower of the Palazzo Vecchio

Brunelleschi designed the great dome of the Duomo, a daring conception that many had condemned as utterly unfeasible, and went on to build several other great monuments: the Spedale degli Innocenti, the Pazzi Chapel, San Lorenzo, Santo Spirito.

Leon Battista Alberti designed the Rucellai Palace and the façade of the Church of Santa Maria Novella; Michelozzo built the Medici- Riccardi Palace; Giuliano da Sangallo left us the spectacu-lar villa of Poggio a Caiano and Benedetto da Majano's masterwork is Palazzo Strozzi.

With the last two great Florentine architects and sculptors, Bartolomeo Ammannati and Bernardo Buontalenti, Florence reached new triumphs of harmony and elegance that included the last restoration of Palazzo Pitti, the Santa Trinita bridge, the jewel-like fountain in Piazza Signoria.

The façade of the Basilica di Santa Croce – one of the greatest achievements of Florentine Gothic art

The Figurative Arts

The beginning of the 13th century also signaled the birth of new, revolutionary modes of painting. Cimabue (1240-1302), the precursor of the Renaissance, was not only a painter; like other painters in Florence, he was also an architect and a sculptor. Cimabue the painter was inspired by the new Romanesque and Gothic monuments in his town. He may even have been involved in the completion of the Baptistry. The subjects of his paintings might still have been under the influence of the old style, but his figures were human, dynamic, free, daringly expressive.

Toward the end of the century, before leaving for Pisa where he had been commissioned to work on the Duomo's mosaics, he established himself as the master of a new school of painting. One of his pupils, Giotto, was destined to become the most famous painter of the next century.

Another great painter of Cimabue's days, Simone Martini, let new ideas permeate his major works, while restricting himself to the framework of traditional Byzantine style. The best example of this is probably his *Annunciation*, which adorns the halls of the Uffizi Gallery, together with several other works by Cimabue and Giotto.

Giotto was not only a great innovator and a very prolific painter, whose work is admired to this day in Florence, Padua, Assisi and elsewhere. While dedicating himself mostly to holy subjects, he rejected old formal bonds in favour of a wholehearted dramatic realism in which his ebullient personality and his great artistry found expression.

A famous anecdote synthesizes clearly Giotto's talent and creativity: while some of his pupils were painfully competing with one another to draw a perfect circle, he swept them aside and, in a single motion, painted a flawless circle, which went down into history as *L'O di Giotto* (Giotto's letter O), an expression used to this day to mean "utmost perfection".

In the fourteenth century painting was greatly influenced by Giotto and his school; among his best known pupils were Bernardo Daddi, Taddeo Gaddi, the Orcagnas and many others. In the field of sculpture we have the works of several great precursors of the Renaissance: Arnolfo di Cambio, Andrea Pisano, Andrea Orcagna and others.

Great monuments required great painters, like Masaccio, the Beato Angelico, Filippo

Leonardo da Vinci carved out of stone

A statue of Donatello

Lippi, Paolo Uccello, Andrea del Castagno, Botticelli, Ghirlandaio and many others. Then there were the sculptors: Donatello, Ghiberti, Luca della Robbia, Verrocchio, Pollaiolo.

Piazza della Signoria is like an outdoor museum of Renaissance sculpture: in addition to the copy of Michelangelo's David, there are several great works by Giambologna (The Rape of the Sabine Women; Hercules and the Centaur), Cellini (Perseus), Donatello (Judith and Olophernes – a copy; the original is inside Palazzo Vecchio) and several others.

Michelangelo and Leonardo, perhaps Italy's major representatives of the Renaissance, also belong to Florence. But during their lifetimes, barely one century later, the Medici court had lost most of its splendor, power and wealth; both of them went to Rome, indepen

Michelangelo Buonarroti in stone

tongue" of the times, Latin. in the second half of the 13th century, things began to happen.

While Giotto was busy painting – and designing his fascinating Campanile (Bell Tower) – the writer Dante Alighieri (1265-1321) created a dialect of the Italian language, the *Dolce Stil Nuovo* (Sweet New Style), born of the Florentine popular speech. Thanks to his master-works – the *Divine Comedy* (*Divina Commedia*), the *Vita Nuova* and the *Convivio*, the Italian language won its place among the great languages of the world.

In Florence, his beloved native city, Dante's name is venerated by all. Walking through the old streets of the city centre, you'll see dozens of stone tablets dec-

dent of each other, to seek their destiny.

Florence has nevertheless always been proud of its two sons who achieved greatness; proud enough, in fact, to have a copy of Michelangelo's *David* erected on Piazza della Signoria, near the entrance to the Palace, with the original occupying a whole alcove (The Tribune of David) at the Academy of Fine Arts (Via Ricasoli 60). Michelangelo's works are also very well repre-sented at the Medici Chapels; and his famous Pietà is the foremost treasure of the Museo dell'Opera del Duomo .

A statue of Dante Alighieri

The Written Arts

The writings of the Middle Ages were scholastic studies, sacred poems, commentaries of the Scriptures and annals, most of them written in the "sacred

orated with verses from his *Divine Comedy,* commemorating the connection between the site and the book. The verses are quoted in Italian, with reference to the source.

Those two contemporary giants, Giotto and Dante, were not isolated phenomena: Dante's famous image, drawn by Giotto himself in the great fresco of the Podestà Chapel at the Bargello National Museum, has beside it other figures which represent almost certainly famous contemporary artists.

Another great philosopher and *literate*, Niccolò Machiavelli, dedicated his genius to structuring the modern state. In his greatest work, *Il Principe*, Machiavelli drew with great prophetic vision the profile of generations of future political leaders: singleminded, dedicated and Machiavellian...

In the world of music, the Ars Nova Florentina of the 13th century, with its innovative conception of vocal and instrumental music, opened the way to the great composers of the European Renaissance and baroque in a great wave of madrigalism, of vocal and instrumental chamber music.

PART TWO – SETTING OUT

How to Get There

BY AIR
Two well equipped airports are in close proximity to Florence and have good public transportation connections to the city:

Amerigo Vespucci Airport, Florence, tel. 055.373.498. Frequent seasonal charter flights from Europe (especially in May, the month of the *Maggio Fiorentino* festival), and several regular domestic flights (from Milan, Turin, Genoa, Venice, Rome, Naples, Palermo etc.). Hourly buses depart from the airport to the *SITA* bus terminal, at 15r. Via Caterina da Siena. The ride takes 15 minutes. For updated timetable information, inquire at the *SITA* information desk, or call tel. 211.487.

Galileo Galilei Airport, Pisa, tel. 050.500.707. Hourly bus connections to and from the Florence Terminal, which is at Santa Maria Novella, tel. 055.216.073. The trip takes close to an hour, with stops at downtown Pisa, Pontedera, Empoli.

BY LAND
By rail or by road, Florence is at the hub of Italy; it lies at the centre of a thick net of minor highways that connect Florence with all Tuscany. Even international express trains connecting Rome with most European capitals make a short stop in Florence.

For railway timetable information, inquire at the Central Station information desk or call tel. 288.785 (opening hours 9am-5pm).

There are several suburban and interurban bus companies; their Florence terminals are generally on Piazza S. Maria Novella, near the Central Station. The most important company is the *SITA*, which has an excellent coach service between Siena and Florence (there is no railway line between the two). For timetable and tariff information, call tel. 483.651 at

Florence, or tel. 204.111 at Siena.

Documents and Customs

Citizens of the European Community may enter Italy freely; the only requirement is a valid document of identity from their own (European) country. Other visitors must have a valid passport or an equivalent document.

As anywhere else in the world, it is highly recommended to come equipped with a health insurance policy. It is recommended that your policy also cover loss and theft of luggage and valuables.

Customs regulations at any port of entrance in Italy allow free import of personal goods at the usual rate of 200 cigarettes, one litre of liquor, 2 bottles of wine and 300cc. of perfume. There are no restrictions on import and export of currency.

When to Come

Florence is particularly charming in the spring, which is also the season of the musical and theatre festival of *Maggio Fiorentino*. In summer, Florence is sometimes very hot, but undaunted tourists nevertheless seem to be all

around town, in the Apennines and at the seaside resorts. A base for touring Tuscany, Florence is at its height in summer.

In autumn, as in spring, the weather is very pleasant. Bad winter weather is not a real problem for the tourist in Florence: with so many museums, churches and palaces to visit, it's possible to keep dry even on rainy days (except for the flooding of the Arno or rare sudden cloudburst).

Holidays

January 1 – *Capodanno*

January 6 – *Epifania*

Sometime in February – *Carnevale*

Sometime in March or April –

Easter, with the famous ceremony of the *Scoppio del Carro* ("blowing up of the carriage")

May 1 – *May Day*

June 2 – *The Day of the Italian Republic*

June 24 – *San Giovanni*, with spectacular fireworks at Piazzale Michelangelo

Seven weeks after Easter – *Pentecoste* (Whitsunday)

August 15 – *Ferragosto (*High Summer Day)

November 1 – *Ognissanti* (All Saints Day)

December 25 – *Natale* (Christmas)

December 26 – *S. Stefano* (Second day of Christmas)

December 31 – *S. Silvestro* (New Year's Eve)

How Long to Stay

A three-day visit is the very minimum needed to see Florence. A day or two longer will make the visit more comprehensive and relaxing.

If Florence is also to be the base for a visit to Tuscany, plan an extra 3-6 days for a charming and fascinating tour in the region.

How Much will It Cost

Surprisingly, Florence is not one of the most expensive towns in Italy; but remember that Italy as a whole is not one of the cheaper countries in Europe.

With accommodation there is a considerable choice: from camping grounds and hostels (under $20 a night per person, with or without what Italians call "breakfast"– bun, jam, butter and coffee), through six classes of hotels. Even the

cheapest pensions will cost at least $40 a night, while the most expensive 5 star establishments may go as high as $400 per person per night, especially during high season. At the tourist class hotels you may expect to spend about $100 a night.

Restaurants are often cheaper at noon than at night; a good but unpretentious restaurant will serve a very satisfactory luncheon for $20-$30 per person; and you might find that one restaurant meal per day is sufficient. There are also many pleasant cheaper eateries that include *pizzerias*, *tavole fredde* ("cold tables" – sandwich bars), fast food and *paninoteche* (sandwich-stands), where you'll be able to make do with as little as $10-$15.

Florence's many museums are expensive, and it is worth inquiring at one of the Tourist Information Offices about "free days" and "daily tickets". If you intend to visit a lot of museums, you should allot $15 a day for entrance fees.

Entertainment can be rather costly, especially if you come in May, during the world famous *Maggio Fiorentino* festival, with its outstanding concerts and operas.

If you plan to use public transportation frequently, you'll need about $10 a day. City taxis are not very expensive (an average ride will cost less than $10). Car rental rates in

Italy are very expensive indeed, over $250 a week for the lowest class car.

As for shopping, Florence's shops are very attractive. Florence's little specialty stores selling leather handicrafts, jewelry, silk and straw are appealing, but don't expect them to be cheap.

What to Wear

Florence is informal (except in the higher class hotels and restaurants, and at gala concerts and opening nights). In summer, even the skimpiest of shorts are acceptable. At night, temperatures may remain quite high and there is seldom need for warmer clothes during the summer months.

In autumn and in spring, it can

be both chilly and wet; some warmer clothes, good shoes, an umbrella and a raincoat are advisable. In winter you will need, of course, even warmer clothes, in addition to standard rain gear.

From June to November, Florence often comes under the attack of great clouds of mosquitoes. In order to protect yourself, either use long sleeves or, better, a suitable repellent.

PART THREE – EASING THE SHOCK: WHERE HAVE WE LANDED?

Transportation

All Florence public buses and trams belong to the *ATAF* network. The *ATAF* information office is at Piazza Stazione, arrivals (tel. 580.528). *ATAF*'s lines cover every nook and cranny of the city.

Most lines operate from the early morning (as early as 5:30am or as late as 7am) and run until close to midnight; however, you'll do well to inquire at the Information Office, especially for the less central lines.

Bus tickets must be purchased before boarding buses (available at most tobacconists and news-stands); they are convalidated by inserting them on your first use of the ticket in the automatic machines situated within the bus itself.

There are various types of bus tickets; plan ahead and buy the type of ticket most suitable for your needs:

– 60 minute ticket; valid for 60 minutes on any number of buses.

– Multiple ticket: a slightly discounted packet of ten tickets.

– 120 minute ticket; very convenient at 150% the price of a 60 minutes ticket.

– 24 hour ticket: a real bargain for frequent bus riders.

– Orange Card: must be used with an identity document; valid for seven days on all buses and local trains.

Lost and Found: via Circondaria 19, tel.367.943.

RADIO TAXI :
Co.ta.fi: via Steccuto 12, tel. 4390.

So.co.ta: via Valdinievole 44c, tel. 4798 or 4242.

CAR RENTAL
We do not recommend hiring a car for use in the city; but for visits to Florence's beautiful countryside and to its many splendid satellites, a car will be a great timesaver. Be forewarned: car rental rates in Italy are very expensive, over $250 a week for the lowest class.

Avis: 128r Borgognissanti, tel. 213.629 and 239.8826.

Europcar: 53r Borgognissanti, tel. 293.444 and 294.130.

Far: 101 Via S. Gallo, tel. 483.410.

Hertz: 33r Via M. Finiguerra, tel. 282.260 and 239.8205.

Maggiore: 31r Via M. Finiguerra, tel. 210.238 and 294.578.

MOTORBIKE RENTAL
Alinari: 85r Via Guelfa, tel. 280.500.
Eurodrive: 48r Via della Scala, tel. 239.8639.
Motorent: 9r Via S. Zanobi, tel. 490.113.
Sabra: 8 Via degli Artisti, tel. 576.256.

Vesparent: 103r Via Pisana, tel. 715.691.

Alinari and *Motorent* also rent bicycles.

Accommodation

As we have already mentioned, there are several hotel-booking agencies in Florence; moreover, the *APT* office has a very complete brochure listing of all hotels in Florence and its district (the brochure contains also other important information).

Official hotel lists aim at a rather rigid "objectivity". They won't go beyond the strict indication of "how many stars" each hotel may have been assigned. However, since accommodation amounts to a very sizable percentage of a traveller's budget, it is important to have additional information on hotels before selecting one.

There are no less than six categories of hotels in Florence. Their prices range from more than $200 per night to as little as $15. Many hotels are

situated in the historic centre, or a few steps away from the railway station.

The price range of the different categories are as follows:
Great luxury – $200 and above
Luxury – $125 and above
Tourist class – $80-120
Economy class – $40-80

HOTEL INFORMATION

Apply for assistance at several information branches if you arrive in Florence without hotel reservations:

Santa Maria Novella Railway Station, tel. 282.893.
Autostrada Firenze-Mare (A11), Service Area Peretola, tel. 421.1800.
Autostrada Sud, Service Area Chianti Est, tel. 621.349.
Fortezza da Basso, tel. 471.960 (April to November).

Some hotel chains also provide information and reservation services:

COOPAL: 2r Prato, tel. 219.525 or 292.192.
Family Hotel: 77 Via Faenza, tel. 490.467.
Florence Promhotels: 72 Viale Volta, tel. 570.481.
CSTM: 6 Via Togliatti, Borgo San Lorenzo, tel. 845.8045.
Youth Hostels Association: 2 Viale Righi, tel. 600.315.
CTS – Students' and Youth Centre: 23r Via Ginori, tel. 289.570.
STS – Students' and Youth Services: 18r Via Zanetti, tel. 288.412.

CAMPING INFORMATION

CNCS – Centro Nazionale Campeggiatori Stranieri: 19 Uscita Autostrada del Sole, Calenzano, tel. 882.391.

GREAT LUXURY HOTELS

Grand Hotel Baglioni: 6 Piazza Unità Italiana, tel. 23580, fax 215.695. The best, very comfortable, just across the street from Santa Maria Novella, very close to the railway station; smart roof restaurant.

Excelsior: 3 Piazza Ognissanti, tel. 264.201, fax 210.278. On one of the best riverside spots, not far from the Station. Breathtaking view from the rooftop restaurant.

LUXURY HOTELS

Brunelleschi: Via dei Calzaiuoli, corner of Piazza S. Elisabetta, tel. 562.068, fax 219.653. In the heart of Renaissance Florence, within a complex of ancient (but very well restored) palaces.

Grand Hotel Majestic: 1 Piazza Ognissanti, tel. 288.781, fax 217.400. Near the Station; often crowded with high class conventions.

Lungarno: 14 Borgo S. Jacopo, tel. 264.211, fax 268.437. A beautiful old palace on the riverside, across Ponte Vecchio, incorporating the 13th century tower of the Marsili family; no restaurant.

Villa la Massa: located at Candeli, 7km east of Florence's historical centre, tel. 055-666.141, fax 055-632.579. A 16th century villa among hills overlooking the Arno River; friendly service; good restaurant.

Bijou: 5 Via Fiume, tel. 214.156, fax 280515. Comfortably close to the Central Station; large, comfortable rooms in a family run friendly establishment.

TOURIST CLASS HOTELS

Balestri: 7 Piazza Mentana, tel. 214.743, fax 239.8042. A wonderful location halfway between Santa Croce and the Uffizi Palace; no restaurant.

Duomo: 1 Piazza Duomo, tel. 219.922, fax 216.410. Smack in front of the Duomo, modest but very convenient.

Sanremo: 13 Lungarno Serristori, tel. 234.2823, fax 234.2269. A small (20 rooms) hotel with a very pleasant lobby and dining room, and attractive rooms; situated on the riverside across the Alle Grazie Bridge, with a view of Santa Croce across the river.

ECONOMY CLASS HOTELS

Aprile: 6 Via della Scala 6, tel. 289147, fax 280.947. Very conveniently close to the railway station.

Astor: 41 Viale Milton, tel. 474.950. Pleasant rooms near the Renaissance centre.

Costantini: 13 Via Calzaiuoli, tel. 215.128. Very reasonably priced. Rather basic rooms, in the best location in town.

Elite: 12 Via della Scala, tel. 215.395. A few paces away from the railway station.

Panorama: 60 Via Cavour, tel. 238.2043. A relatively large hotel not far from Piazza del Duomo.

HOSTELS
Villa Camerata: 2-4 Viale Righi, tel. 601.451 or 600.315. 63 rooms with a total of 400 beds.

Santa Monaca: 6 Via Santa Monaca, tel. 268.338; mostly dormitories.

Camping
Italiani e Stranieri: 80 Viale Michelangelo, tel. 681.1977. Closed November-March.

Villa Camerata (see Hostels, above).

A long list of rooms for rent in private residences is available at the *APT*s.

"Agritourism"
Agritourism is a recent Italian initiative, encouraging small farmers during the high season to become caterers and hoteliers for nature-loving tourists. A night in one of their farms might be a memorable experience – but it could also prove to be a tourist trap.

Driving around Tuscany, you will notice, now and then, an inviting arrow leading to some such authorized farm. Follow your instincts, but in any case remember to view your accommodation before unloading your car!

There is one such enterprise

we are only too glad to recommend:

Il Milione di Brandimarte: Giogoli, 14 Via di Giogoli, Firenze, tel. 204.8713. Leave Florence southward through Porta Romana and after 4km pick the Volterra road; the Giogoli turnoff will be on your right; follow the signs. Unbeatable for its views, its pool, its vineyards, its home-made jams and Chianti wine. They'll frown at a permanence of less than 3 days (there are only 5 apartments and 4 double rooms).

Tourist Information

APT (*Azienda Provinciale del Turismo*) Main Office mailing address: 16 Via Manzoni, Firenze; tel. 23320, fax 234.6286.

APT branches and information services:

15 Via Tornabuoni, tel. 216.544.

36 Piazza Mino, Fiesole, tel. 598.720, fax 598.822.

1r Via Cavour, tel. 276.0382.

17 and 19r Chiasso Baroncelli, tel. 230.2124 or 230.2033.

Piazza della Stazione, arrivals side of the railway station, tel. 212.245.

SOS Tourism, an office of information and assistance (April-October only, 9:30am-12:30pm and 3-6pm) functions at 1r Via Cavour, tel. 276.0382.

Touring Club Italiano, 6r Viale Lavagnini, tel. 474.192.

ACI (Automobil Club Italy), 36 Viale Amendola, tel. 24861.

Tourist guides: 9a Viale Gramsci, tel. 247.8188

Practical Tips

CURRENCY AND EXCHANGE

The Italian currency is the *Lira* (*Lit*). It comes in coins (50, 100, 200 and 500Lit) and in banknotes (1000, 2000, 5000, 10,000, 50,000 and 100,000).

Money is changed at a daily floating rate of change at all commercial banks, upon extraction of a very small fee; most travel agencies, however, charge a rather stiff fee, some-times even higher than 10%, for changing money.

Bank opening hours may vary slightly, but no bank remains open after 4:30pm and all take a siesta break of about 60 minutes from around 1:30pm or so. On Saturday and Sunday all banks remain closed.

WORKING HOURS

Most shops either remain closed on Monday for the whole day, or open only for the afternoon. Saturday afternoon everything closes down, except for public transportation, which operate regularly seven days per week.

TELEPHONES AND POST

Florence's area code is 055.

International calls may be made, using a phone card (available at most newsstands, tobacconists and ticket-counters), from the large majority of public phones.

Italian phone rates are among the highest in Europe, and it might be more convenient, especially for longer calls, to call collect (dial 170) or to limit yourself to the few seconds necessary to give "the other side" the number you're calling from, and wait for them to call you back.

At the public telephone offices one may order international calls, communicate in privacy and pay on the spot. A phone call from your hotel room, like elsewhere, is very costly.

Post Office: 53-5 Via Pietrapiana 53-5, tel. 217.941. Information – tel. 160.

Telephone Booking Office: tel. 214.145. Information – tel. 184.

TIPPING
Most hotels and restaurants will include in their bills both a "cover" (*coperto*) fee and a service percentage (10-15%). Your waiter, however, will gladly accept a personal tip. For espresso it is expected that you leave a small tip on a saucer; coins left by earlier sippers are there to remind you!

ELECTRICITY, WEIGHTS AND MEASURES
Florence runs on 220 volts and 50Hz AC, with rare, self-evident exceptions in some of the older hotels.

The metric system is in use all over Italy.

Clothing and footwear are measured according to the regular European sizes.

The time in Florence, as in the rest of Italy, is GMT+1; in summer, together with the rest of Europe, Italy goes on daylight-saving time.

GETTING TO KNOW FLORENCE

Several separate routes through Florence will take you on a tour of this city of great beauty, built on natural foundations dangerously exposed to the moods of the capricious River Arno.

The first two itineraries lead you through the heart of the ancient streets of the city, within the limits of the original Roman settlement. Beyond this rectangle lie some of Florence's most pleasant grounds and parkland, where there is also much to be seen. The itineraries gradually expand outward, first covering the area north of the Arno river, and then crossing over to the Oltrarno, on the southern side of the river.

These outlying excursions will take you to the Cascine Park and Hippodrome, the northern hills of the Stibbert Museum and Observatory and of San Marco Vecchio. Beyond the Oltrarno, further south of the river, you will visit San Miniato, San Salvatore, the Belvedere Fortress, Poggio Imperiale and Bellosguardo.

Having walked you through most of the city, we'll lead you briefly to the highlights of Florence's green belt and to some of Florence's satellites within a radius of less than 100km. Florence owes much of its character to the charm of its environs. The reddish soil of

Tuscany, the vineyards and olive groves that almost reach the gates of the city, the luxuriant parks and gardens of its many great villas – all these create an atmosphere of pastoral relaxation.

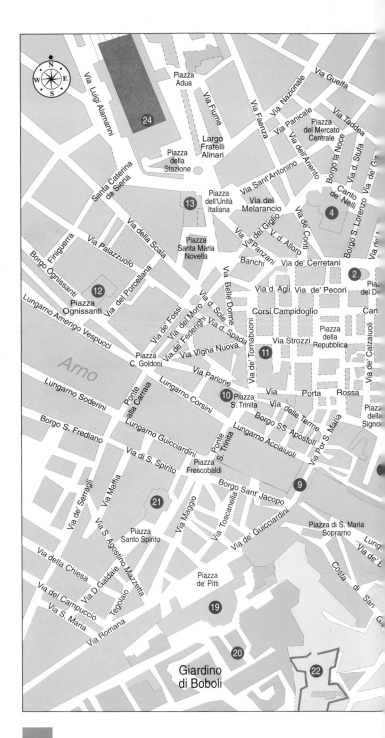

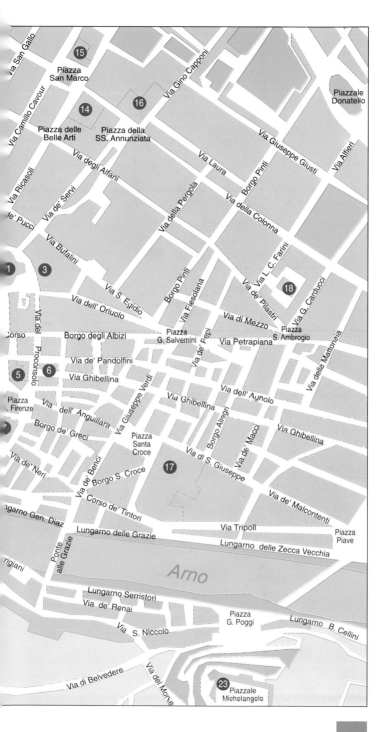

The Heart of the Inner City: From Piazza del Duomo to the Bargello

Looking at the map of the city, one might wonder: is this really a whole day walk? This itinerary covers less than one kilometre, but within it are sites and treasures that will keep you busy from morning to night.

This itinerary is rich in historical sites and great art treasures. Some of the most famous architects, sculptors and painters of the early Renaissance dedicated their life to creating art for the **Piazza del Duomo** complex: Giotto worked on the Baptistry, Arnolfo di Cambio on the earliest stages of the Duomo, Brunelleschi on the great Cupola that bears his name, and scores of other great artists left their imprints in the Duomo, the Campanile, the Battistero, and further on, the Bargello.

The Duomo

The **Duomo** (or Santa Maria del Fiore, or the Cathedral) is an enormous structure, built in the course of more than two centuries, from the late 13th to the middle of the 16th. It rises upon the site of the former Church of St. Reparata. It was commissioned in 1296 by the Republic from Arnolfo di Cambio, who was mandated "to design such a magnificent structure that none better could be conceived by all man's will and might". Arnolfo di Cambio died in 1302, too early to bring his ambitious designs to completion.

Three decades later, in 1334, Giotto was entrusted with the continuation of the project. Giotto was an especially natural choice since he had already designed and built his famous Campanile (belltower). But death once again intervened: Giotto died only

The magnificent Piazza del Duomo, with the Baptistry, the Campanile and the Duomo

three years later, in 1337, and the construction was slowed down.

The newly appointed *Opera del Duomo* administration next commissioned two great architects, Lapo Ghini and Francesco Talenti, to build "the largest and most beautiful cathedral in Italy".

The team of architects, which by then included no fewer than four members, planned and designed for nine years (from 1357 to 1366) until their final proposal was accepted. The four also supervised the construction. By 1378 the walls of the main nave had been completed.

The tribune and the central structure (though not the dome) were ready in 1421. The design of the dome was considered such a grand undertaking that a contest was held among all Florence's leading architects. The winner was Filippo Brunelleschi, whose design seemed to many to be so daring that it was feared that the dome "would bury its builders alive".

Nevertheless, Brunelleschi's design won; the magnificent dome, as we know it today, was completed in 1434. Two years later

Pope Eugene IV consecrated the temple, dedicating it to Santa Maria del Fiore. Much remained to be done on its interior, and most of Florence's greatest sculptors and painters had a hand in the work which took until the middle of the 16th century.

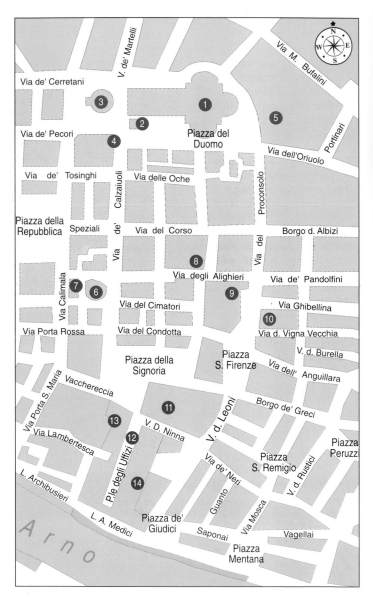

The drawn-out process of constructing the church is clearly visible in the sequence of different, though well integrated, building styles. The majestic front, with its characteristic polychromic marble walls, reminiscent of the Florentine Gothic style, are a late 19th century imitation, inspired by the earlier-constructed side walls and decorations of the Cathedral itself.

Before going in (open daily 9:30am-6pm; entrance free), walk around the great Cathedral, to prepare for the full impact of the interior. The late Gothic and early Renaissance **Porta della Mandorla** (Gate of the Almond), which opens on the northern side of the Duomo, dates from the beginning of the 15th century. Its arch is decorated with the *Annunciation* mosaic by Ghirlandaio. The **Porta dei Canonici** (Gate of the Clergy), on the southern side, dates from the mid-14th century; its panels portray Biblical motifs.

The enormous **dome**, with a diametre of 47m and a height of 114m, is witness to the great genius of its creator, Brunelleschi. The dome's frescos are by Vasari and Zuccari. Those daring to tackle the 464 steps leading to the dome's upper terrace, will find Florence spread out at their feet. The cathedral **crypt** (closed on holiday afternoons) contains fragments of antecedent paleochristian churches and chapels.

THE INNER CITY; THE MEDICI ART HERITAGE

1. The Duomo	8. Casa degli Alighieri
2. The Belltower	9. Badia
3. The Baptistry	10. Palazzo Bargello
4. Loggia del Bigallo	11. Palazzo Vecchio
5. Museo dell'Opera del Duomo	12. Piazzale degli Uffizi
6. Orsanmichele	13. Loggia della Signoria
7. Palazzo dell'Arte della Lana	14. Galleria degli Uffizi

Santa Maria del Fiore is one of the longest churches in the world. It's shaped as a Latin cross, with the imposing Brunelleschi dome at the hub. Having stepped inside, stop for an instant; the first impression is one of almost ascetic simplicity, so different from the immediate sense of awe generated by other great churches.

The greatness of this building is that it imparts a feeling of harmony, of almost musical continuity between the naves, the vaults, the massive yet slender-looking great pilasters, the flowing arches and the gallery; several domed chapels line both sides of the transept.

Your attention will immediately be drawn to the stained glass windows, attributed to Lorenzo Ghiberti, Agnolo Gaddi and other early 15th century artists.

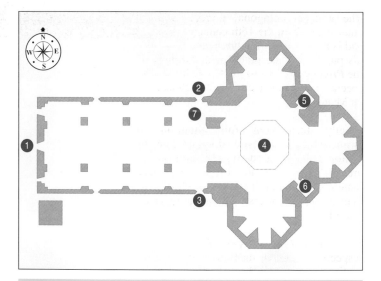

DUOMO

1. Main entrance
2. Porta della Mandorla
3. Porta dei Canonici
4. Choir
5. New Sacristy
6. Old Sacristy
7. Entrance to the dome's steps

Next turn your eyes to the floor, a poly-chromic marble creation composed of several square elements which lead to the main space, just beneath the dome. The floor is attributed to Baccio d'Agnolo and to Francesco da Sangallo and dates from the late 16th century.

At the end of the main nave a great 14th century mosaic by Gaddo Gaddi dominates the whole wall. The 16th century *Angels Praying* frescos are by Santi di Tito, and the *Heads of Prophets* frescos are attributed to Paolo Uccello (1443). Noteworthy among the various busts and funeral statues are those of Giotto (by Benedetto di Maiano, 1490), and of Brunelleschi (by Andrea Cavalcanti, 1447).

The unusual octagonal marble choir dates from the 16th century and is attributed to Bandinelli and his pupils. It is decorated with carvings of the *Prophets and Apostles*. Above it rises the spectacular wooden crucifix by Benedetto da Maiano.

Finally, turn your full attention to Brunelleschi's majestic dome (open to visitors 10am-5pm daily). Its dimensions are gigantic: from the tip of the upper lantern to the floor, it is 114m high (higher than most bell towers); the diametre of its drum is 47m.

While Brunelleschi's plan for the dome respected the main imperatives of the Florentine Gothic style, he proceeded to build what no one had dared to attempt before: a double dome, to be erected from the gallery upward, without scaffoldings.

First, the building materials were hauled to the gallery by means of special machines designed and built by Brunelleschi himself. Next, the outer skeletal dome, which hugs and shelters the inner dome, was erected.

Light falls on the space below the dome from a circle of stained glass windows, designed by Donatello, Paolo Uccello, Lorenzo Ghiberti and Andrea del Castagno. Under the dome, the main altar and its carvings are due to Baccio Bandinelli (1555).

Deep within the left-hand transept is the entrance to the New Sacristy, where Lorenzo the Magnificent found shelter on the day of the Pazzis' Conspiracy, when his brother Giuliano was fatally wounded (see "Introduction – History") Above the entrance is an astounding glazed terracotta *Resurrection* by Luca della Robbia, the incomparable terracotta master and sculptor of the Renaissance.

In the left-hand nave there are also several interesting works of art: the *Divine Comedy* and a *View of Florence* by Domenico di Michelino; a statue of *David* by Bernardo Ciuffagni and two outstanding frescos, an *Equestrian Portrait* by Paolo Uccello and a *Soldier at Arms* by Andrea del Castagno.

Il Campanile di Giotto

Leaving the Duomo, turn to Giotto's belltower, known as **Il Campanile di Giotto.** It is a quadrangular Gothic monument, which incorporates the spirit and moods of Giotto's beloved Romanesque polychromy. It is 84m high, and 414 steps lead to the upper platform (open daily 8:30am-7:30pm in summer, 9am-5:30pm in winter, closed on Easter and Christmas; entrance fee).

Giotto began the actual building of his tower in 1334, assisted by Andrea Pisano, who, after the master's death, completed its splendid

basement. The upper stories, which also remained strictly faithful to the original design by Giotto, took several additional years to construct under the direction of Francesco Talenti.

Two cycles of stone carvings decorate the base. Today the original carvings have been transferred for safekeeping to the Museo dell'Opera del Duomo, and what you see within the Campanile are only copies. The 16 statues that fill the upper niches are also copies, and the originals (most of the statues are by Donatello) can also be seen at the Museo dell'Opera del Duomo.

Three upper storeys rise above the basement. The lower two are lighted on all four sides by elegant Gothic double windows, while the upper floor has thryptic lights. Above the third floor is a projecting cornice with a balustrade, behind which one can enjoy one of the most beautiful views of the city and its outskirts.

The **Baptistry**, a Romanesque octagonal structure in polychromic stone, is the third and most ancient component of the Piazza del Duomo complex. It is also one of the most ancient buildings in Florence (open Monday-Saturday 1-6pm, Sunday 9am-1pm; entrance free).

The origins of the Baptistry are not clear. Some believe that its foundations belong to a very ancient chapel, dating from the 5th century. More ancient, Roman remains seem to indicate that a structure of considerable size had stood here, but there are no clues of its nature and function. Others claim that the earliest elements of the Baptistry belong to the Church of St. John which was erected toward the end of the 11th century; Dante, who was baptised here in 1266, mentions the Baptistry in his works as "my beautiful St. John".

The Baptistry, one of the purest examples of Tuscan Romanesque style

Today the Baptistry remains one of the most beautiful and purest examples of the Tuscan Romanesque style; its three doors are masterpieces of this style. The southern door, which dates from the 14th century, was modelled by Andrea Pisano and cast in bronze by a Venetian artist, Leonardo d'Avanzo. Its 28 panels illustrate the life of St. John the Baptist and the allegories of the Seven Virtues. The two sarcophagi that stand beside the door are Roman, dating from the 2nd or 3rd century.

The northern 15th century door is the work of Lorenzo Ghiberti, with the cooperation of Donatello, Paolo Uccello and others; its 28 panels are dedicated to New Testament scenes. The three bronze statues above the portal (*the Baptist, the Levite and the*

Pharisee) are by Gian-francesco Rustici and belong to the first decade of the 16th century.

The Eastern Door is Lorenzo Ghiberti's greatest masterpiece; Michelangelo himself was so impressed with it that he called it "The Door of Paradise". It is partitioned into ten segments, each dedicated to a different Biblical subject.

It's easy to see why such an enterprise required 27 years of work by the master, assisted by several other major artists. Above the door are two statues: *Saint John Baptizing Jesus*, by Sansovino, and the *Angel*, by Spinazzi. By the way, the third bald man from the bottom at the bottom panel is Ghiberti's own self portrait.

The Baptistry – "The Door of Paradise"

Like the exterior walls, the interior walls of the Baptistry have a lower and an upper order, but here the lower order is composed of an elegant Corinthian colonnade, above which runs a narrow lighted gallery.

The walls are covered with polycromic marbles in the purest Florentine Romanesque style. All the detailing is of the utmost, accurate perfection. The *Giudizio Universale* mosaic in the centre is by Cimabue; the 15th century baptismal fount and the tomb are by Donatello and Miche-lozzo.

A relief from "The Door of Paradise"

At the corner of Via dei Calzaiuoli, on the South side of piazza del Duomo, is the **Loggia del Bigallo** (1352); once the site where little orphans and abandoned infants were offered for adoption, today it is a small museum of medieval art (open to visitors Monday-Saturday 2:30-7pm).

In spite of its modest name, the **Museo dell'Opera del Duomo**, is one of Florence's major museums (open Monday-Saturday 9am-6pm, in summer until 7:30pm, closed on Sundays and holidays; entrance fee; tel. 239.8796). The entrance is directly across the street from the northern side of the Piazza, at No. 9 Piazza del Duomo.

The museum contains a large number of sculptures and architectural fragments of the Middle Age, together with several masterpieces transferred here from their former sites within the Duomo, the Campanile and the Baptistry.

Michelangelo's last sculpture, the unfinished **Pietà**, has a little hall all to itself on the mezzanine floor. The astounding *Dancing and Singing Virginal Voices* by Donatello (1433-39) is on the 1st floor, in the Chorus' Hall, together with another world famous singing group by Luca della Robbia.

The 16 statues removed from the Campanile niches and a great number of "minor" works of great interest and beauty can also be viewed here. At least two hours are needed for the visit to this museum.

In Piazza della Repubblica

Leaving the great complex, walk around the Duomo to the corner of the Campanile, and down Via dei Calzaiuoli until you reach Via Speziali. This short and elegant street ends on **Piazza della Repubblica**, a modern square in the heart of medieval Florence. A wide rectangular square, Piazza della

Repubblica was built toward the end of the nineteenth century, upon the site of the Old Medieval Market. Luxury boutiques and inviting cafés, housed in palaces, line the piazza, and a sort of triumphal arch stands at the mouth of Via degli Strozzi.

Proceed from the corner of Via Speziali along Via Calsaiuoli (enjoying the elegant shopwindows on both sides) in the direction of **Orsanmichele**, which is one block away, at the corner of the street of the same name.

At the end of the 13th century, this square Gothic palace was originally a granary and agricultural market. In the 14th century, after a great fire destroyed some of Florence's then most popular churches, it was decreed that the granary should be transformed into a church.

The project was assigned to a team of famous architects, under the leadership of Francesco Talenti. The church was dedicated to St. Michael of the Garden (*San Michele in Orto),* to commemorate the somewhat plebeian origins of the new church; the "garden" changed spots with the "saint", to become known as *Orsanmichele.*

Fourteen Gothic tabernacles on the outer walls of the building replaced the much simpler earlier openings of the granary. In those niches were placed statues of the patron saints of the major corporations. Inside Orsanmichele, the square pilasters are decorated with frescos of the patron saints of the minor corporations. The most striking element in the church is the **Tabernacle**, by Andrea Orcagna, with its rich ornamentation and the remarkable *Scenes of the Life of the Virgin.*

Behind Orsanmichele is the **Palazzo dell'-Arte della Lana**, the seat of the first and most powerful wool-workers guild of republican Florence, from whose ranks rose the *popolo minuto* who led the rebellion in 1378 (see p. 17). Across the street is the minor church of San Carlo dei Lombardi.

Walk a few more steps eastward along Via dei Tavolini, on to Via Dante Alighieri and then detour left into Via Santa Margherita for a pilgrimage to Dante's alleged birth-place, **Casa degli Alighieri** (Via Santa Margherita 1, open daily 9am-12:30pm and 3-6:30pm, closed Wednesday afternoon and holiday afternoons; entrance fee; tel. 283.343). This is a small museum dedicated to the poet, with frequent modern art exhibi-tions on the ground floor.

Follow Via Dante Alighieri until it ends at Via del Proconsolo and turn right to the **Badia.** Nothing remains of the original 10th century church (built by the Countess Wilma, wife of Ugo King of Italy and mother of Ugo of Tuscany) except for the slender Romanesque belltower, whose upper stages flow so harmoniously into a limpid Florentine Gothic style.

Within the church, admire the remarkable Renaissance ceiling due to Matteo Segaloni. Most of the sculptures and carvings are Renaissance works, with the exception of the frescos in the left side chapel, by one of Giotto's pupils. Near the exit is Filippo Lippi's most admired painting, *St. Bernard and his Vision of the Virgin* (1480).

The Palazzo Bargello

Just across the street (Via del Proconsolo) from the Badia is the **Palazzo Bargello,** which houses the **National Art Museum**.

This great fortresslike medieval palace, with its solemn **Volognana Tower**, stands at the mouth of Piazza San Firenze. Built in 1256, almost half a century before the Signoria Palace, it was the first residence of the mayor of Florence.

Walk into the Bargello court-yard, where the seeming disarray adds to its majesty and charm. On three of its sides runs an elegant portico. Above the columns and the arches of that portico scores of carvings in stone, terracotta and marble are inserted. An uncovered stair-case, almost ascetic in its simple lines, climbs along the court-yard's fourth wall to the beautiful first floor *verone,* the elegant balcony built in 1319 by Tone di Giovanni.

One of the statues in the National Art Museum, the most important museum of Renaissance sculpture today

The **National Art Museum** is today the most important museum of Renaissance sculpture (open to visitors Tuesday-Saturday 9am-2pm, Sunday 9am-1pm, closed on Monday; entrance fee; tel. 210.801). In its halls are many "minor" masterworks by Michelangelo, Donatello, Brunelleschi, Ghiberti, Benvenuto Cellini, the Della Robbias, Verrocchio and many less known artists.

No less interesting are the great halls them-selves and the already-mentioned majestic balcony of the first floor, with its delicately decorated arched ceiling. The following is a list of some of the most important master-works to be found in the various halls:

A statue on display in the National Art Museum

The Arms Room, near the palace entrance, contains a collection of the Renaissance arms and armour of the Medici family.

A door in the courtyard leads into the Thir-teenth Century Room (see the *Virgin with Child* by Tino di Camaino), and then to the Michelangelo Room. The master stairway leads into the General Council Room, dedi-cated to Donatello and his school of art. The Majolica Room, the Ivories Room and the

PIAZZA
DI S. FIRENZE

Vestibule lie beyond. The frescos of the Podestà Chapel are attributed to Giotto.

Don't miss the Cellini Room, the Della Robbia Room and the Verrocchio Room on the second floor.

A few steps away from the Bargello and the Badia, Via del Proconsolo ends at Piazza San Firenze. On the south-western corner of this square stands the 15th century Palazzo Gondi, a princely mansion by Sangallo. The palace across the square, between two twin late baroque churches, is the seat of the Courts of Law (which have lately expanded also to one of the two churches).

Here, only a few steps away from Piazza della Signoria, is where you can find one of Florence's best restaurants, *Il Bargello* (at No. 4; tel. 214.071; closed on Tuesday). Here ends the first itinerary through monumental Florence, and begins our next itinerary.

A view from the Campanile

The Medici Art Heritage: From Piazza della Signoria to the Uffizi Gallery

Having taken in the majesty and splendour of Florence's architectural treasures on Piazza del Duomo, we'll now acquaint you with Florence's major art trove in an even more concentrated tour of the Uffizi Gallery.

The majestic Piazza della Signoria

This second itinerary focuses around what was, in the days of the Signoria, Florence's hub of political power – Piazza della Signoria. The majesty of the palaces surrounding the great square and the statues that decorate it only hint at what lies within the walls of what was the administrative centre of Florence during the Medici's rule: the Uffizi Gallery.

This unforgettable museum houses the very best of what the Italian Renaissance – and first and foremost Florence – contributed to humankind in the short span of five generations

Piazza della Signoria was designed in the 13th and 14th century on the grounds of former pro-Emperor *Ghibellini* palaces, which were razed to the ground after the victory of the pro-Pope *Guelfi* faction (see "Introduction – History"). This majestic square soon became the hub of Florence's political and social life, and was appropriately embell-ished with allegoric statues representing some of Florence's most beloved symbols: the *Marzocco*, Florence's famous lion, *Judith and Olophernes* (Donatello), *David* (a copy – by Michelangelo), *Cosimo I* (by Gianbologna), the *Fontana del Nettuno* (by Ammannati) and *Ercole e Caco* (by Bandinelli).

The Palazzo Vecchio offers visitors tremendous artistic riches

In the middle of the square, the spot of Girolamo Savonarola's execution is marked. Savonarola (1452-1498) was a rebellious friar, with a compulsive vision of social reform. He was excommu-nicated by the Pope and sentenced to death at the stake by Florence's civil courts of law on May 23, 1498.

The square is dominated by the great mass of the **Palazzo Vecchio** (which is open to visitors Tuesday-Friday 9am-7pm, Sunday 8am-1pm, closed on Saturday and Monday; entrance fee; tel. 276.8465). This is an early 14th century castle-like, severe palace, designed by the great Arnolfo di Cambio, who modelled it on the Guidi Castle at Poppi.

Built in the age of the "castle-mansions" when all palaces of the great families sport-ed a tall, proud tower at one of the corners. Palazzo Vecchio's specimen (*noblesse oblige!*) is 94m tall.

While the front of the palace and its tower are rigidly Gothic, the inner court is a Renaissance jewel, brilliantly designed to harmonise perfectly with the earlier Gothic frame by Michelozzo Michelozzi and deco-rated by Vasari.

A staircase climbs to the **Quartieri Monu-**

mentali, where the Medicis used to hold court among Michelangelo's statues and Vasari's paintings.

The walls of the main hall, called **Salone dei Cinquecento** (Hall of the Five Hundred), are covered with a series of frescos depicting the battles of Cosimo I. The 39 ceiling panels are also covered with frescos; here Vasari escaped the irksome task of painting with a chronically upturned head by leaving the actual job to his pupils.

The Palazzo Vecchio as seen from the interior

The walls of the other great hall, the **Sala dei Duecento,** (Hall of the Two hundred) are covered with magnificent Florentine tapestries. The adjacent little **Study of Francis I** is a delicious den, designed and decorated by Vasari himself.

A small door, to the left of the entrance, leads to the **Medicis' Rooms**, each of them dedicated to one of the members of the great family. On the second floor you'll find a suite of elegantly frescoed rooms, leading to the **Apartments of Eleanor of Toledo,** consort of Cosimo I. Here Vasari outdid himself: the four rooms of the apartment are of indescribable aristocratic grace.

A passage leads into the **Cappella della Signoria**, where, among its rich frescos and paintings, Girolamo Savonarola spent his last night in prayer before his execution. The stairs back at the passage lead to the top of the tower. On a clear morning the view is breathtaking and well worth the climb.

At Piazza della Signoria

Piazza della Signoria ends, on its south side, with **Piazzale degli Uffizi**, a

The narrow Piazzale degli Uffizi, enclosed by the Loggia della Signoria and the Palazzo degli Uffizi

narrow rectangular square practically enclosed by two majestic buildings: the Loggia della Signoria (or Loggia dell'Orcagna) on the western side and the Palazzo degli Uffizi on the eastern side, both designed by Vasari. The *piazzale* ends at the river.

The **Loggia della Signoria** was originally, at the end of the 14th century, a meeting place of Florence's leading families. Today, it is a great art gallery, rich in Renaissance paintings and sculptures. The *loggia* is yet another example of how Florentine architects succeeded in magically blending styles, which enhanced the harmony of the whole. Here there is a rare blend of Late Gothic and Early Renaissance, born of an original design by Orcagna. The *loggia* also goes by two other names: *Loggia dei Lanzi* (since it was the headquarters of the *Landsknechts,* the company of German soldiers serving as Guards of the *Signoria*) and *Loggia dell'Orcagna.* Under the *loggia* are several statues and sculptures, some of them Roman, others Florentine Renaissance works. Don't miss Benvenuto Cellini's *Perseus* in the left arch.

At the Galleria degli Uffizi

The **Palazzo degli Uffizi** was built to serve as the Medici's administrative centre. Its two floors contain the richest and most important collection of paintings and sculptures in Italy, the **Galleria degli Uffizi** (open Tuesday-Sunday 9am-7pm, holidays 9am-1pm, closed Monday; entrance fee; tel. 218.341).

The majestic staircase, corridors and halls are a museum within a museum. The first floor is dedicated to a collection of 50,000 drawings and 60,000 prints; the second floor corridors, decorated with Flemish and Florentine tapestries, lead to the two main galleries of paintings. The **East Gallery** has no fewer than 24 halls.

The first three contain early Renaissance works by Florentine painters (Cimabue, Giotto, Duccio di Buoninsegna and Simone Martini). Among the most salient works in other halls are the portrait of *Federico IIda Montefeltro* by Piero della Francesca (Hall 7), two *Madonnas* by Filippo Lippi (Hall 8), *Portrait of a woman* by Pollaiuolo (Hall 9); Botticelli claims most of the next five halls; in Hall 15 you'll see masterpieces by Perugino and Leonardo (*Adoration of the Magi, Annunciation*).

The interior of the Galleria degli Uffizi, which contains the most important collection of sculptures and paintings in Italy

The octagonal Hall 18 contains mostly portraits. The last halls contain, together with other works of the Italian Renaissance, some famous paintings by exponents of other great schools: Dürer, Cranach, Holbein, El Greco and others. The last "masterpiece", at the end of the corridor, is the breathtaking view of the city and Ponte Vecchio as seen from the loggia's terrace.

The **West Gallery** (20 halls) contains works by Michelangelo (*Sacra Famiglia*, Hall 25), Raphael (*Madonna del Cardellino*, Hall 26),

Titian (*Flora*, Hall 28), Andrea del Sarto, Veronese, Tintoretto, Guardi, Canaletto, Tiepolo, Rubens, van Dyck, Rembrandt and many others.

In May 1993 a bomb was detonated by terrorists in the heart of the Uffizi Gallery, causing severe damage to several works of art, most of which were later restored with great accuracy.

Since a visit to the Uffizi takes several hours, it constitutes a whole itinerary in itself, and here ends our second tour of Florence.

If you are hungry, try the rustic *Trattoria Antico Fattore*, 1r Via Lambertesca, just behind the Loggia della Signoria (tel. 261.215; closed Sunday and Monday). It specialises in authentic popular local dishes, like *pasta e ceci* (ceci-chickpeas), *ribollita* (a meat and vegetable soup), and a rich selection of beef and other meats.

Art in Piazza della Signoria

A Lungarno Promenade: From Ponte Vecchio to Santa Maria Novella

There is much more to monumental Florence than Piazza del Duomo, Piazza della Signoria and the Galleria degli Uffizi. Other places that shouldn't be missed include Ponte Vecchio, Ognissanti and Santa Maria Novella.

Ponte Vecchio and other bridges on the River Arno

Ponte Vecchio is little less than a legend which has survived, practically unchanged, for more than six centuries, with the characteristic ranks of small boutiques and the splendid views of the riverside *Lungarni* avenues and of the whole city.

Ognissanti is a street and a square, indeed almost a quarter; here, in the days of Florence's great splendour, many great Florentine families built vast and elegant mansions and palaces, comfortably close to the centre of town and to the refreshing riverside.

Finally, Santa Maria Novella is one of the most prestigious churches of medieval and Renaissance Florence. It's also comfortably close to the railway station, the bus terminal, scores of tourist hotels, as well as the *APT* Tourist Information Office.

We start our itinerary at **Ponte Vecchio**. Nothing is known of the original bridge, except that it existed during Etruscan times.

We don't know if it withstood the wars and floods of the Roman Era; we do know that a new wooden bridge was built over the river in 972 which lasted for more than three cen-

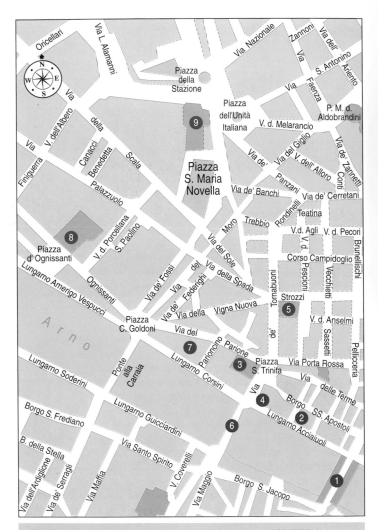

FROM PONTE VECCHIO TO SANTA MARIA NOVELLA

1. Ponte Vecchio
2. Chiesa de' Santi Apostoli
3. Chiesa di Santa Trinita
4. Palazzo Spini Ferroni
5. Palazzo Strozzi
6. Ponte della Trinita
7. Palazzo Corsini
8. Chiesa di Ognissanti
9. Chiesa di Santa Maria Novella

turies, until the great flood of 1333. Those were the days of Florence's greatest wealth. In 1345 Neri di Fioravante was appointed to launch across the river "a great unshakeable bridge to be admired by all Florentines and their guests".

Fioravante's design included a triple archway bridge, wide enough to bear a double row of public shops along its sides. The design was approved, the bridge was built, and the shops were granted, in the beginning, to the powerful Butchers' Guild. The butchers' cartel lasted until the days of Cosimo I de Medici, on whose orders the butchers were ousted and silversmiths and goldsmiths took up shop in their stead.

Ponte Vecchio by night

These small shops have become a landmark of Florence, for which even the Nazis showed respect. In 1944, bent on their work of destruction, they blew up all Florence's bridges except for Ponte Vecchio; the bridge was left whole, save the two ranks of shops at its ends, which suffered damage.

The street leading to Ponte Vecchio from Piazza della Signoria is Via Por Santa Maria; *Por* is short of *Porta* (Gate); this is where one of the gates in Florence's medieval walls, the Santa Maria Gate, once stood.

Approaching the bridge from this street, you'll see above the shops, on the left side, a long, interesting covered corridor that runs from the Uffizi Gallery to the Palazzo Pitti. This is the **Vasarian Corridor**, an elegantly simple structure well worthy of the great architect's genius (visits by appointment only, tel. 23885; Tuesday to Saturday

from 9:30am; entrance fee included in the Uffizi Gallery ticket).

The silversmith shops run from both sides of the bridge almost to its middle. At the very centre of the bridge itself, above the top of the central arch, the Vasarian corridor continues, but the shops disappear, leaving the view over the river open on both sides.

Standing beside the bust of Benvenuto Cellini, the famous Florentine Renaissance sculptor (an early twentieth century work by Raffaele Romanelli), and looking out to the right (downriver) you'll see the beautiful Trinita Bridge and the two Lungarno (riverside) strips. On the left side (upriver), the Lungarnos are framed by the hill of San Miniato.

The bust of Benvenuto Cellini on Ponte Vecchio

Having strolled by the silversmith workshops, walk away from the bridge and into Lungarno Acciaiuoli, walking toward the Santa Trinita Bridge. Turn into the third alley on your right, and you'll come to the little **Chiesa di Santi Apostoli**. This is a very ancient church, built in the 11th century like the Baptistry and San Miniano. It was remodelled twice during the Renaissance, and finally restored to its original Florentine Romanesque design. The simple, relatively unadorned interior, has a main nave and two lateral aisles, forming an interesting semi-circular apse. Left of the apse is a terracotta *Tabernacle* by Giovanni della Robbia. Near the tabernacle is the Tombe of Oddo Altoviti, a member of one of Florence's oldest families, by Benedetto da Rovezzano.

The narrow side streets (between Borgo Santi Apostoli and Via delle Terme) are flanked by minor Medieval palaces and mansions. Some of them are characteristic *tower houses*, though lacking the majesty and splendour of Palazzo Vecchio.

Turn left into Borgo dei Santi Apostoli

toward **Piazza Santa Trinita** (although in Italian the stress in the word *"Trinita"* should be on the "a", here in Florence the first "i" in this word is stressed). In the middle of the square stands a granite column that used to belong to the Roman Caracalla baths; it was presented to Florence, and to Duke Cosimo I, by Pope Pius IV. The red marble statue of *Justice* is by Tadda (1581).

The **Chiesa di Santa Trinita** is an 11th century Florentine Gothic structure, rebuilt in the 12th century and extended again in the 13th. Its front which dates, however, from the late Renaissance, is by Buontalenti.

The inner chapels and many of the frescos and paintings in the interior date from the 14th century. There are many important works of Renaissance painting, of which the most interesting are a vivid *Trinity,* the *Stories of Mary,* the *Figure of the Prophets* (by Lorenzo Monaco), an *Annunciation,* the *Miracles of St. Francis, Views of Florence* and a dramatic *Crucifixion.*

The ancient Chiesa di Santi Apostoli

Near the front of the Santa Trinita Church you'll see a pleasant statue (by Giovanni Caccini, a 16th century pupil of Giambologna), which according to legend represents St. Alexis, a 4th century wealthy Roman scion, canonised after having lived a life of penitence and poverty with two miraculous interventions of the Virgin Mary.

Another legend tells that Cosimo I Medici, who had the great granite column erected in the middle of the square, was able to do so only after consulting with an unknown stranger who solved for him a seemingly impossible problem of gravity. When the stranger's idea proved viable, Cosimo wanted to thank him; but the stranger had disappeared; the sculptor Caccini was ordered to erect a statue in honour of this stranger.

The **Bartolini-Salimbeni Palace**, just off the square, is one of the earliest examples of Baccio d'Agnolo's architectural style, developed to cater to the whims of 14th century "*nouveau riche*" families.

In fact, such a wave of criticism was aroused that Baccio felt it necessary to respond to the critics by boldly engraving a latin inscription over the main door of this palace: *Carpere Promptius Quam Imitari* ("It's easier to criticise than to copy"). Baccio's (and other architects') later works indicate that his critics lost their cause. Another example of Baccio's school of architecture is the **Spini Ferroni Palace**, near Piazza Santa Trinita, with its majestic three stories and its crenellated top.

Higher up along Via dei Tornabuoni, at the corner of Via degli Strozzi, is the **Palazzo Strozzi**, one of Florence's Renaissance jewels. Its simple, almost monastic elegance

does not diminish the first impression of great wealth and power it evokes. It was built in the late 15th century by Benedetto di Maiano to serve as the residential palace of the great Strozzi family, one of the Medicis most stubborn opponents.

The Strozzis were finally exiled by their Medici opponents, and their palace remained unfinished in the back to this day. The inner courtyard, with its colonnade and upper lodges, is by Simone del Pollaiolo, also known as Cronaca.

Turn back toward the river until you reach the **Ponte della Trinita** (Bridge of the

Trinity). The original bridge was built by Ammannati in 1570, and was destroyed by the Nazis during their 1944 retreat, together with the rest of Florence's bridges (except for Ponte Vecchio). The present reconstruction is faithful to Ammannati's design.

The only original elements of the bridge are the allegoric statues of the Four Seasons, situated at the corners of the bridge. When the Germans blew up the bridge, the statues fell into the river, and a special team of underwater experts were able to find and recover all four when the bridge was rebuilt. The head of "Spring", however, was missing. The whole city wept at the loss. Rich prizes were offered for the return of the head; finally, in 1961, during routine work on the river, the head was found and restored to its original place.

The building to the left of the bridge (our backs to the bridge) is the three story **Palazzo Spini Ferroni**, which is a fine example of a typical wealthy medieval home.

Don't cross the bridge, but rather walk halfway to its middle for an exceptionally good view of Ponte Vecchio, and then proceed along Lungarno Corsini. At the

Lungarno corner with the narrow Via Pari-oncino you will see another elegant mansion, the 17th century **Palazzo Corsini** (by Antonio Ferri), which inspired scores of European architects of that epoch.

The palace's first floor contains the **Art Gallery**, a private museum rich in very valuable works by Raphael, Signorelli and other Renaissance artists.

Don't miss the **inner courtyard,** a jewel of its style. The entrance to the palace is at 11 Via del Parione (tel. 287.629; by appointment only)

Back to the river, continue toward Piazza Goldoni, with Ponte alla Carraia on your left. This is another bridge that had to be rebuilt after having been blown up by the Germans during World War II.

From the Piazza, proceed to Borgo Ognissanti (the first street off the river across the square), and walk to Piazza di Ognissanti. The house at 12 Borgo Ognissanti is known to Florentines as the "Upside Down House" (*casa alla rovescia*). Notice that the supports of its terrace and the balustrades of both terrace and windows seem to have been set in place upside down.

The **Piazza di Ognissanti** is a mixture of Renaissance and later styles. The statue in the middle is *Hercules fighting the Lion*, an early 20th century neo-classic work; the three major buildings on the square are two large luxury hotels (the *Excelsior* and the *Grand Hotel),* and the 15th century **Palazzo Quaratesi**.

At the far end of the piazza from the river stand the **Chiesa di Ognissanti** (All Saints

Church). It's yet another composite style church: of the original 13th century structure only the **Belltower** remains; the rest was utterly rebuilt in the 18th century. Inside, the 17th century dominates the scene, while the side chapels are strictly Renaissance.

In the interior, the frescos are by Ghirlandaio and by Botticelli, who is buried here; a marble plaque marks the spot on the floor. The second chapel on the right is decorated with a fresco of the Vespucci family; most probably the youngster whose head appears between the Virgin and the old man is Amerigo Vespucci, the Florentine explorer to whom the continent of America owes its name.

Beside the Ognissanti Church, at No. 42 in the Refectory (open Monday, Tuesday and Saturday 9-noon; entrance free; tel. 239.6802) is Domenico Ghirlandaio's Last Supper (1480), a great painting which was much admired by Leonardo da Vinci.

Coming up from the river along Via del Porcellana, at your back is the beautiful Renaissance **Loggia di San Paolo,** whose portico is decorated with terracotta medallions by Giovanni della Robbia and a marvellous lunette illustrating *St. Dominic and St. Francis,* by Andrea della Robbia.

Before you is the beautiful gardenlike **Piazza di Santa Maria Novella**, with its two majestic marble obelisks, erected in the early 17th century to serve as markers for the *Palio dei Cocchi* (a traditional carriage race).

A marble obelisk at Piazza di Santa Maria Novella

erected in the early 17th century to serve as markers for the *Palio dei Cocchi* (a traditional carriage race). Walk across the square to the beautiful **Chiesa di Santa Maria Novella**, built by the Dominicans in the 13th and 14th centuries.

In this church, too, many great Florentine architectural styles have been integrated into a whole of great intrinsic harmony. The bell-

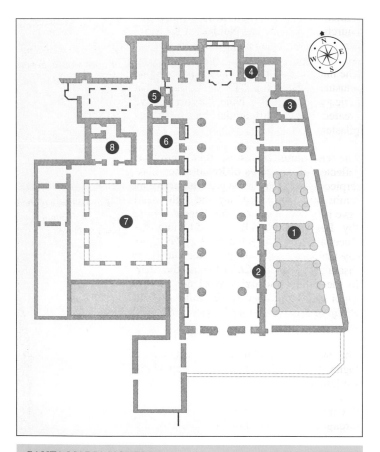

SANTA MARIA NOVELLA

1. Noblemen's Cemetery
2. Monument of the Blessed Villana
3. Rucellai Chapel
4. Filippo Strozzi Chapel
5. Strozzi Chapel
6. Sacristy
7. Green Cloister
8. Spanish Chapel

Jacopo Talenti: an elegant, slender example of pure Lombard Gothic style.

It took most of a century for the façade of the church to become what it is today. Sedate Florentine Gothic elements with Romanesque undertones characterize its lower parts. Above the great architrave section is Alberti's Renaissance contribution, flanked by two *Astronomical Instruments* by Ignazio Danti, Cosimo I's court astronomer. Along the right hand wall of the church is the ancient **Noblemen's Cemetery,** enclosed by an elegant colonnade.

A detail on a building at the Piazza di Santa Maria Novella

The interior, subdivided in three naves in the unusual shape of a "T" cross, has great majesty and beauty. Note the perspective created by the differential spacing of its pilasters.

The enormous riches of this church is reflected in the scores of Renaissance masterpieces as well as in the great luxury of its tombs and chapels. Along the right hand nave is the *Monument of the Blessed Villana* (by Bernardo Rossellino, 1451) and the Rucellai Chapel, with the *Tomb of Fra'Dati* (by Ghiberti, 1425) on the floor and Nino Pisani's *Virgin with Child* behind the altar. In the Filippo Strozzi Chapel are Filippo Lippi's frescos *Story of St. John and St. Philip* and Benedetto da Majano's *Tomb of Filippo Strozzi*.

The belltower of the Chiesa di Santa Maria Novella

The main altar's Crucifix is by Giambologna. A second Strozzi Chapel, deep within the left side nave, is decorated with a series of 14th century (restored) frescos by Nardo di Cione; its altar table is by Andrea Orcagna. Another famous Crucifix by Brunelleschi is in the first chapel of the left side nave.

The wooden chorus is decorated with frescos by Ghirlandaio (the famous *Stories of Mary*) The sacristy contains

a terracotta basin by Giovanni della Robbia and yet another marvellous *Crucifix* (designed by Giotto) and Masaccio's incomparable masterwork, the *Death* fresco (1428).

Along the left outside wall of the church is the unusual complex of the **Chiostri** (Cloisters)**.** The first is the **Green Cloister,** a Romanesque style great hall, designed toward the middle of the 14th century by Fra' Giovanni da Campi, probably as the first section of a Dominican Monastery. It owes its name to the hues of its great frescos, *Scenes from the Old Testament,* by Paolo Uccello.

A small door in the far wall of the Green Cloister leads into the little, jewellike **Spanish Chapel**, the Chapter Hall of the Monastery. It's easy to spend at least an hour admiring the great frescos of this chapel: the *True Penitence* cycle by Andrea Bonaiuti, the *Triumph of St. Thomas Aquinas,* the *Saints Confronting the Heretics* and many others.

Inside the Chiesa di Santa Maria Novella

Walk out of the Santa Maria Novella Church, following its eastern walls to **Piazza dell'Unità Italiana**, next to the railway station (Stazione Santa Maria Novella). Cross this square into Via del Malarancio, and stop for a last admiring look, from a different angle, of this great majestic church.

To end this itinerary, walk back to the square and toward the river along Via de' Fossi, with its interesting antique shops. From Piazza Goldoni turn right to *Harry's Bar,* on 22r Lungarno Vespucci (tel. 239.6700), either for a classic (not inexpensive) *pasta* dinner, or for a pleasant *café* along the river.

The Piazza and Chiesa di Santa Maria Novella

The Northern Inner City: Museums, Churches and Galleries

Even though San Lorenzo is barely a stone's throw away from the Duomo, we didn't include it in the Duomo route because its spectacular cloisters and chapels need to be given the honour of their own tour.

Several other great museums and monuments are included along the route that follows the north-eastern limits of the Old City. At San Marco you will discover one of the first and most captivating early Renaissance painters, Il Beato Angelico. Michelangelo's *David* stars at the prestigious Galleria dell'Accademia and many other great works of art are on display at the Pinacoteca of the Spedale degli Innocenti.

The route leads us to one of Florence's most harmonious squares, Piazza della Santissima Annunziata. After visiting the Museo Archeologico, the tour ends at Florence's Synagogue, with its modest museum.

The **Chiesa di San Lorenzo**, one of the greatest monuments of Florence's early Renaissance, is about half way between the Duomo and Santa Maria Novella, where the last walk ended.

The first chapel erected on this site was consecrated in the year 393 by Milan's great

Saint, St. Ambrose. In the early 11th century, the chapel was replaced by a large Romanesque church. The glories, wealth and ambitions of Florence and the Medicis were growing so swiftly, that the church soon seemed not large enough, not splendid enough. Filippo Brunelleschi was therefore commissioned by Cosimo il Vecchio de' Medici to design and build a new church.

Filippo Brunelleschi submitted his design in the early 15th century and the church was completed in 1460 by one of his pupils, Manetti. The front of the building, however, has remained unfinished to this day.

The interior of the church is divided into three naves by two rows of elegant Corinthian columns.

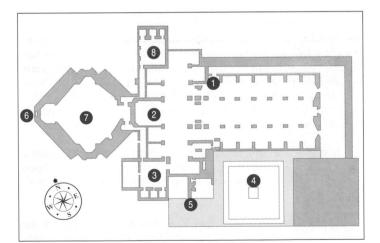

SAN LORENZO

1. Donatello pulpits
2. Main Altar
3. Old Sacristy
4. Brunelleschi's Cloister
5. Laurentian Library
6. Entrance to the Medicis' Chapels
7. Princes' Chapel
8. New Sacristy

The central nave, far wider than the two lateral ones, is lighted by rectangular windows, enhancing the beauty of its ceiling panels and of the geometric patterns in the

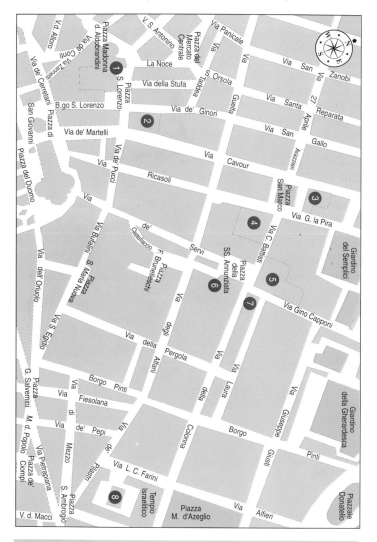

THE NORTHERN INNER CITY

1. Chiesa di San Lorenzo
2. Palazzo Medici-Riccardi
3. Museo di San Marco
4. Galleria dell'Accademia
5. Chiesa della Santissima Annunziata
6. Spedale degli Innocenti
7. Archeological Museum
8. Synagogue

marble floor. The lateral naves are somewhat darker; the light that filters through their little round windows emphasises the cross-vaulted lines of the ceiling.

At the far right end of the central nave are the two world-famous pulpits by Donatello, whose panels illustrate *The Passion of Christ*. Don't miss the *Deposition* on the left side pulpit, which is the last (and one of the most eloquent) works of that great artist. A few steps from the pulpit, near the right end of the central nave, you'll see the interesting *putti* (statues of infant angels) by Desiderio da Settignano, the greatest master of this art.

The **Main Altar**, enclosed within a balustrade, is decorated with semi-precious stones. The crucifix is by one of Michelangelo's pupils, Baccio da Montelupo. Under the metal gratings Cosimo il Vecchio (the Elder) is buried; next to him lies Donatello, who was one of Cosimo's most beloved artists.

Stroll along the side walls of the church; there are several great frescos by "minor" Renaissance painters, like Bronzino (*The Martyrdom of San Lorenzo)*, Annigoni (*St. Joseph and the Child*) and many others. San Lorenzo has two sacristies: the first, by Brunelleschi, is on the left; on the right side is Michelangelo's own New Sacristy, which belongs to the complex of the Medicis' Chapels (described below).

Brunelleschi's **Old Sacristy** is a jewel-like square structure, delicately lighted through the lantern of its little dome and through the lunettes on the side. Its altar is attributed to Donatello's school. Donatello himself left us the magnificent decorations of the cloister's columns, its tympanum, its bronze doors and the bust of San Lorenzo (in terra-cotta, on the right cabinet).

The great sarcophagus in the middle of the cloister, with the bodies of Giovanni de' Medici and his wife Piccarda, is by Andrea Cavalcanti. The red marble and bronze sarcophagus is by Verrocchio, and it contains the remains of Cosimo the Elder's sons Giovanni and Piero.

Before leaving the church, pause for an instant at the **Martelli Chapel**, nesting near the left side pulpit, and admire Filippo Lippi's *Annunciation* above its altar. A brief staircase leads to the first floor porch, from which you'll enjoy a beautiful panoramic view of the San Lorenzo complex.

Now turn left at the church entrance and into the narrow corridor that runs along the left

side of the church; cross the beautiful **Brunelleschi's Cloister** to the **Laurentian Library** (open 9am-5pm; closed for maintenance during the first half of September; entrance free; tel 210.760). The library building, designed by Michelangelo, reflects the majesty of his genius. Cosimo the Elder, and later his grandson Lorenzo the Magnificent, had collected a vast treasury of ancient manuscripts, parchments and art works; and encouraged by Pope Clement VII, Lorenzo had Michelangelo erect the Library's monumental seats and staircase.

Just behind the church, on Piazza Madonna degli Aldobrandini, is the entrance to the remarkable **Cappelle Medicee** (Medicis' Chapels, open to visitors Tuesday-Sunday 9am-2pm, closed on Monday; entrance fee; tel. 23885). Cross the vast cryptlike space and climb the staircase to the octagonal **Princes' Chapel** (by Nigetti, based on a design by one of Cosimo I de' Medici's

Feeding the pigeons

son). It is a Mausoleum of the later Medici princes and it leads into the halls of the **Museo dell'Opera Medicea Laurenziana**, a very minor museum of religious art by Florentine standards.

From the Princes' Chapel we pass on to the **New Sacristy**, in which Michelangelo kept to the frames dictated by Brunelleschi in his "Old Sacristy", injecting them with his own unique vision of the Renaissance, in which the first hints of the baroque influence are reflected.

The two incomparable **Sepolcri Medicei** (Medicis' Tombs) are a superb collection of Michelangelo's sculptures: the bust of Duke Lorenzo of Urbino (*Il Pensieroso*), with the images of *Dawn and Sunset*; and across them, those of *Day and Night* lying upon the tomb of Duke Giuliano of Nemours; the statue of the *Madonna with Child*, behind the altar, is also by Michelangelo, while the two saints at her side are by Montorsoli and Raffaello da Montelupo.

Left of the chapel apse is a small, lower hall decorated with several wall drawings by Michelangelo and his school (entrance limited to small groups of less than 12 persons; reserve your place beforehand, at the Chapels' entrance).

After the visit to the San Lorenzo complex, return to Piazza San Lorenzo. At the corner of Via de' Gori and Via de' Ginori stands the **Palazzo Medici-Riccardi** (open 9am-1pm

Classic art on display at the Gallery of the Academy

and 3-6pm, holidays morning only, closed on Wednesday; entrance fee; tel. 276.0340), a superb specimen of the Florentine Renaissance style, built by Michelozzo (1444-1464) to serve as Cosimo the Elder's residence. Lorenzo the Magnificent made it his own royal residence; today it is the seat of the Regional Government (*Prefettura*).

Its harmonious inner courtyard leads into an Italian style inner garden and to the **Chapel**, specially famed for its Benozzo Gozzoli frescos which illustrate the splendour of Florence at the peak of the Medicis' glory. The baroque **Gallery** is frescoed by Luca Giordano. The palace houses also the **Museo Mediceo** (draperies, documents and Filippo Lippi's *Madonna*), the **Biblioteca Riccardiana** (tel. 212.586) and the **Accademia della Crusca**, founded for the compilation of the Italian Vocabulary.

From the Palazzo, continue on Via de' Gori, and at the first street turn left onto Via Cavour (rather than right to Piazza del Duomo), strolling along the eye-catching shopwindows to Piazza di San Marco. On this Piazza is the **Museo di San Marco** (open to visitors Tuesday-Saturday 9am-2pm, Sunday and holidays 9am-1pm, closed on Monday; entrance fee; tel. 23885), actualy situated within the complex of what used to be in the Middle Ages St. Mark's Convent.

Cosimo the Elder, who was not only a very wealthy but also a very devoted prince, undertook the restoration of the old monastery that was practically falling apart. Michelozzo, Cosimo's favourite architect, was charged with the great project, and soon the renovated convent acquired great prestige.

The great painter Beato Angelico was born in a little village at the gates of Florence in 1387; he became a friar at the age of 20 and was allowed to devote himself to the art of painting. He won great fame from his Orvieto and Vatican frescos, and was rewarded by the Pope and by the city of Florence by being made Prior of St. Mark.

After his death he was canonised by the church, and became known as "Il Beato Angelico". The convent itself survived as such for almost four centuries, until 1860, when it became property of the State. Today it is a museum dedicated mostly to the work and life of Beato Angelico.

Also in the museum, in the former **Ospizio dei Pellegrini** (pilgrims' hospice), are the *Final Judgement*, the *Coronation of Maria* and other masterworks; in the tabernacle are the *Madonna della Stella* and the *Madonna dei Linaiuoli*; in the Capitular Hall is the *Crucifixion* and on the top of the staircase is the first *Annunciation*.

Most upper floor cells are deco-rated with Beato Angelico's frescos, among which two other *Annunciazione* in the 1st and 3rd cells). *The Last Supper*, in one of the dining halls, is by Ghirlandaio. The *Giudizio*

The statue of Ferdinando I de' Medici, at the Piazza della Santissima Annunziata

Finale in the main dining hall is by Fra' Bartolomeo.

Particularly beautiful in its pastoral purity is the **First Cloister**, with its grassy garden and its great Cedar of Lebanon. Under the elegant colonnade there are many marble inscriptions, lunettes and a series of 16th century frescos, illustrating the life of St. Antoninus.

On the upper floor, at the end of the corridor, are the cells where Girolamo Savonarola used to live, and to whom most art works in the cloisters are dedicated.

The **Chiesa di San Marco** belongs to the same vast complex, and it used to be the chapel of the old Dominican convent. It contains several important works of art, among which a *Crucifix* attributed to Giotto and the mosaic of the *Virgin in Prayer*, dating from the 7th century. A detailed inscription under the mosaic tells the story of this great masterwork. It seems that the Riccis, a medieval aristocratic dynasty that settled in Florence during the 12th century, had the mosaic brought over from one of Rome's oldest churches, Santa Maria Antiqua, and affixed here in their own family chapel.

Light penetrating the Chiesa della Santissima Annunziata

Standing just in front of St. Mark's and looking toward the square, you'll see on your left three great complexes: the first, and closest to you, are the **Natural Science Museums** (Via La Pira 4, Tuesday-Saturday 9am-1pm; entrance fee). This complex, which belongs to the Florence University, is composed of

The Gallery of the Academy – a corridor leading to the Tribune of David

the Museum of Geology and Paleontology (tel. 238.2711, closed also on Friday) and the Museum of Mineralogy (tel. 216.936).

The second palace belongs to the University Campus. The third, and by far the most important of the three, is the **Gallery of the Academy** (Galleria dell'Accademia; Via Ricasoli 60, open to visitors Tuesday-Saturday 9am-2pm, Sunday and holidays 9am-1pm, closed on Monday; entrance fee; tel. 23885). The Gallery is an absolute must, if only because its **Tribune of David** is the site of the most famous statue of the Renaissance: the world famous *David* by Michelangelo.

But there is much more to be seen in the Academy's halls: medieval and Renaissance paintings of the Florentine school, several sketches by Michelangelo, the so-called *Palestrina Pietà*, also by Michelangelo, and the originals of the sculptures that decorate Piazza della Signoria.

Walk into Via Cesare Battisti, that runs between the University Palace and the Gallery, and you will soon reach **Piazza della Santissima Annunziata.** With its spectacular colonnade by Sangallo, the two striking baroque fountains and the statue of

Chiesa della Santissima Annunziata

A fountain in Piazza della Santissima Annunziata

Ferdinando I de' Medici (by Giambologna, 1608), this is probably the most harmonious square in the whole city.

The Romanesque **Chiesa della Santissima Annunziata** (tel. 239.8034) and the Spedale degl'Innocenti (the Innocents' Shelter) form a majestic complex, situated on the narrower northern side of this square.

The church was originally built in the 13th century by the Servi family, rebuilt by Michelozzo in the 15th century and later restored several times. It contains several great works of art by Renaissance and baroque artists. Above the altar stands the venerated image of the Virgin, sketched, according to legend, by an unknown 13th century painter who fell into slumber while painting, only to discover, upon awakening, that the image had been miraculously completed by an angel.

The **Spedale degli Innocenti** (open to visitors Monday-Saturday 9am-7pm during the summer, and 9am-1pm in winter and on Sunday and holidays; entrance fee) is one of the earliest and most original Florentine Renaissance monuments, with a splendid colonnade by Brunelleschi and a series of terracotta *putti* by Andrea della Robbia. In its **Pinacoteca** (painting gallery; same opening hours; tel. 247.9317) you'll find paintings by Ghirlandaio (*Epifania*), Neri di Ricci (*Incoronazione della Vergine*), Philipo Lippi, Piero di Cosimo etc.

The next door **Archeological Museum** (Museo Archeologico; open to visitors Tuesday-Saturday 9am-2pm, Sunday and holidays 9am-1pm, closed on Monday; entrance fee; tel. 23575) is of particular interest for the study of Etruscan life and culture. It also possesses several rare Greek, Roman and Egyptian artifacts. There are also interesting collections of ancient coins and jewels.

Back at Piazza della Santissima Annunziata, follow via della Colonna to Piazza d'Azeglio. Here, turn right at Via Farini, to the attractive church-like building of the **Synagogue**, and its small museum (4 Via Farini, tel. 245.252). It was built in neoclassic style, at the end of the 19th century.

The Synagogue, built in neoclassic style

The synagogue was built to replace two former little synagogues that had been set up in the Ghetto, an area established in 1571, defined as the streets between Piazza della Repubblica and Piazza dell'Olio. The emancipation of the Jewish community of Florence began in the second half of the 18th century, under the rule of the Lorraine Grand Duke. In 1881 the Ghetto was razed to the ground; only a stone tablet commemorates its site today.

The Jewish presence in Florence was never a factor of great importance in the life of the city. The first few Jewish families were money-lenders, who were invited by the Medicis in the 15th century. The Jewish Community began to grow after the expulsion of the Jews from Spain (1492), and in the beginning of the 20th century it numbered almost 3000 people. During World War II 250 were killed, and many left Florence after the war. Today there are 1200 members in the community.

The nearby *Cuscussu* restaurant (2a Via Farini, tel. 241.890) is Florence's only Kosher restaurant. But if you not looking for kosher food, and are willing to spend what it takes for a princely meal, go back on Via Farini to Piazzale d'Azeglio to one of the most sophisticated restaurants in Florence, *Relais le Jardin* (Piazza d'Azeglio 5, tel. 245.247, closed Sunday). The restaurant, attached to the *Regency Hotel*, serves excellent French and Italian cuisine.

The green dome of Florence's church-like Synagogue

The Oltrarno and its Pearl –
The Palazzo Pitti

This walk is centred around Florence's most imposing and largest Renaissance palace, which houses half a dozen great museums (all of them are closed on Monday); if the palace is to be granted its due, there will be little time to see anything else during this day.

In the immediate vicinity of the great palace are several major Oltrarno monuments which cannot be overlooked; Santa Felicita is one of Florence oldest churches and the Chiesa del Santo Spirito is one of Florence's richest.

Finally, just behind the complex of the Palazzo Pitti and its Boboli Gardens, stands the imposing Belvedere Fortress, also known as St. George.

Ponte Vecchio is a very convenient starting point for this tour, close to the heart of Monumental Florence and to the Galleria degli Uffizi (and to the entrance to the Vasarian Corridor which leads to the Palazzo Pitti itself).

Having crossed the bridge, follow Via Guicciardini. On your left, a few steps from the bridge, you'll be at Piazza Santa Felicita. The little **Chiesa di Santa Felicita** is one of

the oldest in Florence. It stands on the remains of an even older cemetery, and was built in the 11th century as the first parochial church of the Oltrarno. The most important treasure of the church is the *Deposition* by Pontormo; you'll find it within the first chapel on the right. Evidence of several later restoration works during the Renaissance and once more in the 18th century are visible.

Further on along Via Guicciardini, pause briefly before the **Palazzo Serristori** and

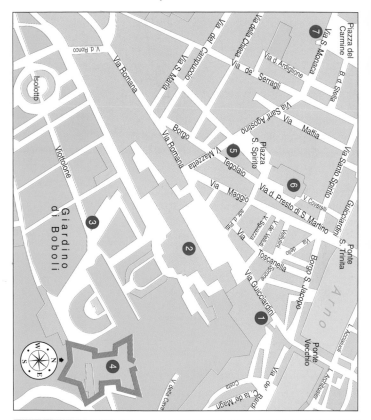

THE OLTRARNO

1. *Chiesa di Santa Felicita*
2. *Palazzo Pitti*
3. *Boboli Gardens*
4. *Fortezza del Belvedere*
5. *Palazzo Guadagni*
6. *Chiesa del Santo Spirito*
7. *Chiesa di Santa Maria del Carmine*

carry on to Piazza de' Pitti, enclosed on three sides by the magnificent complex of the Palazzo Pitti. It was designed by Brunelleschi, who had been charged by the proud Pitti family to "erect for them Florence's most imposing palace", which he proceeded to do.

Luca Pitti was a fabulously rich merchant – and a great rival of the Medicis. He had asked Brunelleschi to design windows that should be "greater by far than the entrance gate to the Medici-Riccardi Palace" in Via Cavour. Brunelleschi accepted the challenge and, while following strictly the imperatives of his own Renaissance style, he created a simple but majestic three floor giant, the **Palazzo Pitti**.

The Pittis' financial empire, however, crashed before the completion of the building. Ironically, almost a century later, in 1549, the unfinished giant was purchased by Eleanor of Toledo, Cosimo I's consort; she had the palace completed by Bartolomeo Ammannati, who was able to express his own architectural genius without offending Brunelleschi's style. Eleanor also hired the great garden architect Tribolo, who transformed the hilly grounds behind the palace itself into a magnificent park, that became known as the **Boboli Gardens**.

Cosimo I had the great architect Vasari build the corridor that bears his name, to lead from the Palazzo Uffizi to the Palazzo Pitti, crossing the river above the eastern side of Ponte Vecchio. The two lateral wings date from the 17th and 18th centuries.

The great palace was the official residence of the Medici and the Lorraine Grand Dukes, and briefly, when Florence was the capital of the Kingdom of Italy (1865-1871), it was the Italian Royal Palace. Today it houses the Palatine Gallery, the Argenti Museum and the Gallery of Modern Art.

A lavishly decorated hall in the Palazzo Pitti's Palatine Gallery

Walk into the majestic front door, which opens into Ammannati's vast **courtyard.** From the courtyard, straight ahead is the so-called *Moses' Cave.* Above it, upon its terrace, stands the graceful *Artichoke Fountain*. Through the cave one can reach the Boboli Gardens (see below).

On your right is the staircase that leads to the **Palatine Gallery** (open Tuesday-Saturday 9am-2pm, Sunday and holidays 9am-1pm, closed on Monday; entrance fee; tel. 238.8611), on the first floor. On the same floor are, on the left, the 28 great halls of the Gallery (not all of them are open to

visitors). The right side of the floor contains the 17 even larger rooms of the Royal Apartments.

Besides the sheer size of the palace, the brazen opulence of each and every hall, their shining marble floors, the frescoed walls and ceilings, and the gilt doors leave no doubt that only the richest of the rich could have dreamed up this monument to wealth.

The Gallery contains more than 500 great masterpieces, most of them from the 16th and 17th centuries.

The list is very impressive indeed: Titian, Rubens, Tintoretto, Andrea del Sarto, Salvator Rosa, van Dyck, Raphael, Caravaggio, Ghirlandaio, Velazquez, Aretino and Pontormo, to name some. A map and illustrated catalogue of the Gallery is on sale at the ticket office.

We shall point out a few "musts": in the first hall, **Hall of Venus** (Sala di Venere) you'll find two pieces by Titians (*The Concert* and *Beauty*), as well as a Venus statue by Antonio Canova. Raphael's *Veiled Woman* is in the **Hall of Jupiter** (Sala di Giove); in the **Hall of Saturn** (Sala di Saturno) you'll see several other Raphael masterpieces (among which the *Grand Duke Madonna* and the *Madonna of the Chair*).

The royal **Appartamenti Monumentali** (Monumental Apartments; tel. 238.8611) also contain a number of 17th and 18th century paintings. They are fully furnished in the most elegant Neo classic style.

The second floor contains the **Modern Art Gallery** (Galleria d'Arte Moderna; same opening hours as the Palatine Gallery; entrance fee; tel. 287.096); in its 30 great halls are representatives of Tuscan art from the end of the 18th century to the present.

A ceiling in the Palazzo Pitti

On the left of the courtyard, in the summer apartments of the Grand Dukes and in the mezzanine floor, is the **Silver Museum** (Museo degli Argenti; open Tuesday-Saturday 9am-2pm, Sunday and holidays 9am-1pm, closed Monday; entrance fee; tel. 294.279). It has a wonderful collection of

In the Boboli Gardens

precious objects: gold, silver, precious stones, crystals, ivory etc. Particularly interesting are the precious stone vases belonging to Lorenzo the Magnificent's collection, the cameos and medallions of the Medicis and the silver plates from Augsburg (16th and 17th centuries).

Before going into the Boboli Gardens, the **Meridian Pavilion** (visits by appointment at the Uffizi Gallery; tel. 23885) beckons, with yet another 11 sumptuous halls of 16th and 17th century paintings forming the **Contini-Bonacossi Collection** (which will be transferred to a new site; updated information is available at the Uffizi Gallery). The pavilion also hosts the **Costume Museum** (open on Tuesday, Thursday and Saturday 9am-2pm, closed holidays), with scores of original costumes worn by the Florentine aristocracy.

The Fortezza di Belvedere

The **Boboli Gardens** (tel. 213.440) are laid out on the open spaces that spread and climb to the sedate hillside behind the great palace (open daily 9am-6pm in summer, 9am-5pm in winter; entrance free). The gardens were planted and stylised by the Medicis, only after they bought the Palazzo Pitti in the middle of the 16th century. Opened to the public in the 18th century, the magnificent park is a fine example of Renaissance-style gardens, with good views of the palace, the river and the whole city.

Walk through the left *rondo* of the palace or through the courtyard and the *cave*. There are several interesting spots: the **Buontalenti Grotto** (1588) with its statuary and gallery, the 17th century **Amphitheatre** and *Neptune's Statue* and *Pool*. The best observation point is near the hill top, at the *Knight's Garden*. The apparently modest little villa beside it contains the **Porcelain Museum** (open on Tuesday, Thursday and Saturday 9am-2pm), with three halls of 18th century European porcelain. The elegant *Ocean Fountain* is by Giambologna.

The massive walls of the Fortezza di Belvedere

High above the Giardino di Boboli, just beyond the garden's north-eastern corner, stands the **Fortezza del Belvedere**. The fort was built by Buontalenti for the Pitti family, and its name hints at the sights one enjoys from its ramparts – outstanding views of Florence and its surrounding hills.

After visiting the Pitti-Medici kingdom, return to the Piazza de' Pitti. The narrow Sdrucciolo de' Pitti, a very steep alley that begins at the front of the Palazzo, brings you to Via Maggio, whose many palaces built along it are from the Medici days, when it was a most popular avenue for the upper class.

At Via Maggio turn left, and walk to its end,

The Chiesa del Santo Spirito

at Piazza di San Felice. A right turn to Via Mazzetta brings you to the **Piazza di Santo Spirito**, with its surrounding *palazzi* and market. Two buildings dominate this *piazza* – a palace and a church.

At the corner of the Via Mazzetta and the square is the **Palazzo Guadagni,** the admirable Renaissance palace with its magnificent porch (*loggia*), designed by Cronaca (1503).

The **Chiesa del Santo Spirito** (Church of the Holy Ghost) is one of Brunelleschi's latest works. Its limpid, simple but elegant Renaissance front is a welcome change from the overpowering pride of the Palazzo Pitti.

The church contains 38 little chapels, each with its own art treasure. On the left side of the end wall, stop for an instant to admire Ghirlandaio's pupils' beautiful *Nativity*. In the third chapel on the left side of the church, the *Statue of Christ* is a 16th century copy of a Michelangelo work; the original is in Rome, in the Church of Minerva.

From the square continue into Via Sant'- Agostino and then Via Santa Monaca to the **Chiesa di Santa Maria del Carmine**. Of the original Romanesque structure, which was almost obliterated by fire in 1771, two chapels survived, the Cappella Corsini and the Cappella Brancacci (on the right arm of the "T" shaped church).

The **Brancacci Chapel** (open to visitors Wednesday-Monday 10am-5pm, holidays 1-5pm, closed on Tuesday; entrance fee; tel.

238.2195) contains some of the most expressive and beautiful Renaissance frescos in Florence, a true saga of frescos by Masolino di Panicale, his great pupil Masaccio and Filippo Lippi. Don't miss *The Temptation of Adam and Eve* (on the extreme right, upper panel), *The Payment of the Tribute* (centre left, upper panel) and the *Expulsion of Adam and Eve from Eden* (extreme left, upper panel).

Our tour ends here. If you are hungry, take a short walk to 6r Via Santo Spirito, to taste some of the best vegetarian food in Florence at the *Cantinone del Gallo Nero* (tel. 218.898).

The view of Florence from the Fortezza di Belvedere

Southern Hills and Monuments: From Santa Croce to San Miniato al Monte

This itinerary requires good weather, not only because it's a rather long walk, but because it would be a pity to miss the views of the city as seen from Piazzale Michelangelo and from San Miniato al Monte.

This route takes you beyond the limits of the monumental historic city, to the green hills of the southern banks of the Arno where one of Florence's greatest art treasures, the Church of San Miniato al Monte, resides.

The starting point is **Piazza di Santa Croce**, one of Florence's landmarks. Its vast open space is dominated by the majestic church of Santa Croce. Across the square from the church are several Renaissance palaces; the most eye-catching (at No. 1) is the **Palazzo Cocchi Serristori**, built in the late 15th century by Baccio d'Agnolo. Also interesting is the multi-colored front of the **Palazzo dell'Antella.**

Dominating the Piazza is the great Gothic church, **Chiesa di Santa Croce.** While the bell tower and the façade are a 19th century

The great Church of Santa Croce

reconstruction, the church is still one of the greatest achievements of the Florentine Gothic style. It was built upon the remains of an ancient Franciscan chapel in the first half of the 14th century by Arnolfo di Cambio and his pupils.

Stop for an instant to look at the façade. High above the main entrance, in the upper triangle is a six-pointed star, better known as the "Star of David", which is one of the symbols of Israel and Judaism; it was inserted here by the architect appointed by the City in 1860 to plan the façade. Unbeknownst to the City Fathers, the architect, Niccolò Matas, was a Jew. The significance of the symbol was apparently unrecognized by the townsmen, and this is why, to this day, a Star of David dominates the front of the Church of Santa Croce.

The Gothic interior of the Chiesa di Santa Croce

Santa Croce has traditionally been the burial ground for Florence's elite (more than 280 have been granted this honour to this day). It contains, among other, the tombs of Machiavelli (between the fourth and fifth altars in the right nave), Michelangelo (the tomb by Vasari, in the right nave), the 19th century composer Gioacchino Rossini (also in the right nave), Galileo Galilei (in the second altar in the left nave), and Ugo Foscolo and Vittorio Alfieri (two great Italian poets of the early nineteenth century).

The six-pointed Star of David which dominates the front of the Church of Santa Croce

Santa Croce draws its majesty from the simplicity and the elegance of its two slender colonnades and their elegant Gothic arches. The ceiling is scaffolded, but its walls are covered with frescos by Giotto and his pupils,

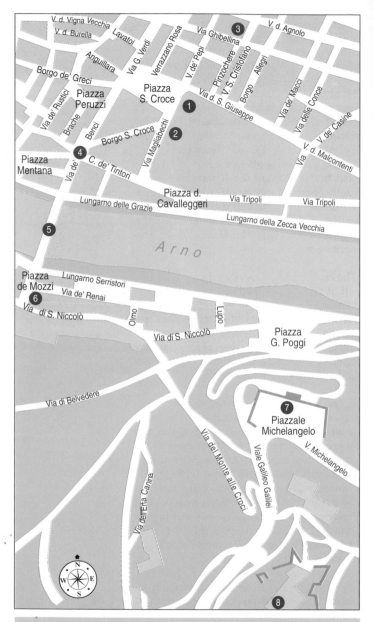

FROM SANTA CROCE TO SAN MINIATO AL MONTE

1. Chiesa di Santa Croce
2. Pazzi Chapel
3. Casa Buonarroti
4. Museo Horne
5. Ponte alle Grazzie
6. Museo Bardini
7. Piazzale Michelangelo
8. San Miniato al Monte

Regrettably, Cosimo the Elder, who held in little regard the achievements of earlier artists, had all the frescos whitewashed and almost utterly destroyed. The few surviving fragments are kept in the Santa Croce Museum (see below). Other 14th century frescos have survived within some of the church chapels, the **Castellani** or Sacrament Chapel (with the fresco *Stories of the Saints* by Agnolo Gaddi), the **Baroncelli,** now Giugni Chapel (with *Stories of the Virgin*, also by Gaddi) and the **Rinuccini Chapel** (with *Stories of Mary Magdalene, of the Virgin Mary*, the *Saviour* and the *Four Evangelists*, by an unknown 14th century artist, rightly nicknamed "The Master of the Rinuccini Chapel").

The Belltower of the Church of Santa Croce

The church has no less than 14 side chapels. All of them at one time belonged to some of Florence's greatest families, serving as their private cemeteries. Most of the frescos that grace them have been more or less successfully "restored" in the course of the centuries; several of them were unfortunately damaged beyond repair.

In the **Santa Croce Museum** (open Thursday-Tuesday 10am-12:30pm and 3-6:30pm, in winter only until 5pm, closed on Wednesday; entrance fee; tel. 244.619) there are, in addition to the above-mentioned fresco fragments from the church walls, a crucifix by Cimabue, and *San Ludovico*, a bronze statue (*St. Ludwig of Toulouse*) by Donatello, other frescos by Taddeo Gaddi, a collection of 16th and 17th century paintings. Many of the works kept here were severely damaged by the great flood in 1966.

Along the right side wall of the church is the **Santa Croce Cloister**, a magnificent 14th century courtyard, with on its left side (along the church wall) an elegant colonnade that leads to the front of Brunelleschi's **Pazzi Chapel.** This chapel was the latest work of that great architect, who died in 1446, before completing the chapel. The

The massive Church of Santa Croce rises above the surrounding buildings

entrance to the chapel, simple and modest, is undoubtedly one of the purest examples of the early Renaissance style in Florence.

Having left the church, turn, at the corner of Piazza Santa Croce, into Via dei Pepi. The second street on your right is Via Ghibellina, where, at No. 70, you'll find **Casa Buonarroti** (open Wednesday-Saturday and Monday 9am-2pm, Sunday and holidays 9am-1pm, closed on Tuesday; entrance fee; tel. 241.752). This is not, as the name would indicate, the home or birthplace of Michelangelo (he was born in a small village near the town of Arezzo), but rather the house he bought for his nephew, one Leonardo Buonarroti.

Casa Buonarroti

For almost three centuries the house remained in the hands of the family, until 1859, when it was given as a gift to the city, to be turned into Michelangelo's sanctuary and private museum. Since 1964, Casa Buonarroti has also been the seat of the **Michelangelo Study Centre**. The whole house is dedicated, of course, to Michelangelo's life and work. The two lower floors contain several early works, a bronze statue of the artist by Daniele da Volterra and even the famous *Portrait of Vittoria Colonna,* probably by Pontormo. The upper floor is reserved to the Michelangelo Study Centre.

Walk back to Piazza di Santa Croce, and this time walk to Via dei Benci, turning toward the river. At the corner of Corso dei Tintori, inside a 15th century palace (by Cronaca), is another little museum, **Museo Horne** (Via Benci 6, open Monday-Friday 9am-1pm, closed Saturday and Sunday, entrance fee, tel. 244.661). The Horne Museum is furnished as a 15th century patrician residence, and contains a valuable collection of paintings, including *St. Stephen by* Giotto.

A room in Casa Buonarroti

Continue a short walk along the Via de' Benci to the river, and to the **Ponte Alle Grazie**, a 13th century work which was reconstructed after World War II. Walk about half-way on the bridge itself and pause to catch the beautiful view of Ponte Vecchio, the Vasarian Corridor and the complex of Palazzo Vecchio and the Uffizi. Two great monuments are also visible from here across the river: the imposing (even from its back side) Palazzo Pitti and the Church of the Holy Spirit.

Cross the bridge to the *Oltrarno* side and to Piazza de' Mozzi. On your left, at the corner of Via de' Renai, is the **Museo Bardini** (open Monday Saturday 9am 2pm, Sunday

and holidays 9am-1pm, closed on Wednesday; entrance fee; tel. 234.2427), whose 20 halls are dedicated to ancient, medieval and Renaissance sculptures in wood, bronze, marble and terracotta; there are also several important Renaissance paintings and furniture, an armoury and Persian carpets of the 16th and 17th centuries.

The marble façade of San Miniato al Monte

Leaving the museum behind, follow Viale G. Poggi toward Piazzale Michelangelo and San Miniato al Monte. The best time for this walk, with some of the most charming views of Florence, is the early morning; however, it's advisable to preserve your strength and catch a ride up – either by taxi or by bus, at least as far as Piazzale Michelangelo.

Here, on the square itself, there is an observatory terrace with a fascinating view of Florence. The Michelangelo munument on the square is a 19th century effort, created with bronze reproductions of the artist's most famous statues.

A statue in the Monastery of San Miniato al Monte

High above Piazzale Michelangelo, and well behind it, rises **San Miniato al Monte**, the most remarkable monument of the Florentine Romanesque style, built during the 11th and 12th centuries. Its harmonious multi-coloured marble façade, which has been admired and studied by generations of art and architecture students for its unique balance and harmony, dates from the 11th-13th centuries.

The interior is divided in three naves; the marble floor of the central nave dates from 1207, and ends with Michelozzo's **Chapel of the Crucifix** (1448). Don't miss the magnificent fresco in the apse (*The Blessing of*

Christ between Mary and San Miniato). There are also many fragments of frescos by Paolo Uccello. The sacristy frescos (*Scenes of St. Benedict's life*) are by Spinello Aretino.

On the right side of San Miniato stands the crenellated **Bishops' Palace** (Palazzo dei Vescovi), which was built in the 14th century. Beyond the palace, within the fortress' walls (built by Michelangelo in 1530), there is Florence's **Monumental Cemetery of the Holy Gates**.

San Miniato al Monte

Florence's Green Belt

Florence is framed by a belt of luxuriant, green rolling hills covered with vineyards and olive groves and peppered with ancient monasteries, churches and villas.

At the main bus terminal just outside the railway station you'll find buses to most of the sites around the city. The main highlights of this chapter are the Cascine, the Stibbert Villa and Museum and the Certosa del Galluzzo. Note that these sites comprise more than just one itinerary.

For an off-the-beaten-track route, take a bicycle tour of Green Florence, along the outer fringes of the monumental quarter of the city and the northern bank of the Arno. To hire a bicycle, contact the *Motorent* Agency at 9r Via San Zenobi (tel. 490.113).

Le Cascine

A pleasant public park, it is popular among Florentine lovers and young families, and very crowded on sunny Saturdays and Sundays. Situated west of the city centre, on the slopes of a hill that ends at the riverside, **Le Cascine** is less than 2km away from the railway station (*ATAF* bus line 17). Meadows and woodland, avenues and secluded pathways, tennis grounds, swimming pool, hippodrome and many other facilities are available. On Ascension

In Le Cascine Park

Day, Le Cascine hosts the popular traditional music and song festival of the *Festa del Grillo* (the Cricket's Festival).

La Certosa del Galluzzo

Galluzzo is a modern village situated less than 6km south-west of Florence. Its main claim to fame is its medieval **Certosa**, which rises at the gates of the village, upon a picturesque hilltop covered with olive and cypress trees (*ATAF* bus line 36 from the main bus terminal, near the railway station, or drive southward along the A1 Autostrada "Certosa"; guided tours every half hour 9-noon and 4-7pm in summer, 3-5pm in winter; small contributions welcomed; closed on winter Tuesdays, tel. 204.8876). This monastery was built in the 14th century. The vast Certosa complex includes the **Church of San Lorenzo**, the **Palazzo degli Studi**, an **Art Gallery** and the **Monastery**. The museum displays works by Della Robbia, Pontormo and other pre-Renaissance and Early Renaissance artists.

The Stibbert Villa, Park and Museum

Bus No. 1, which may be boarded at any of several stops in the centre of town, will take you northward 3km to Via Stibbert, which ends at **Villa Stibbert**, with its Belvedere (observatory), park and museum. The attractive park is very popular and may be rather crowded, especially on the sunnier weekends. The 60 halls of the great villa are somewhat haphazardly furnished in a mixture of styles. The monumental villa and vast garden belonged to an early 19th century adoptive Florentine Englishmen and a compulsive art collector. On his death, Stibbert left all his properties and art collections to the City of Florence. Of particular interest is an unusual series of leather tapestries, collected by Stibbert on his voyages. The villa's halls are crowded with medieval arms and armour, terracotta and china artwork, and costumes and paintings, which together form a unique though haphazard museum (open Friday to Wednesday 9am-1pm, closed on Thursday; entrance free; guided tours every half hour; tel. 475.520).

The Abbey of San Salvatore in Settimo

12km south-west of Florence (*ATAF* line 26 from the main bus terminal) is the very fine old **Church of San Salvatore**, which has a beautiful Romanesque façade with Gothic overtones and a striking belltower. Near the church are the ruins of an old Abbey, often frequented in sunny week-ends by romantic young lovers.

Green Florence by Bike

A very pleasant bicycle route along a special lane starts at **Porta al Prato**, at the eastern end of the Cascine. It follows Viale Belfiore, passing behind the Railway Station to the enourmous walls of **Fortezza da Basso**, with its **Belvedere** and its gardens. The route follows the walls of the fort eastward along Viale Strozzi and Viale Spartaco Lavagnini to **Piazza della Libertà**.

Here one may take a short way – following Viale Matteotti to the **Giardini della Gherardesca**, Viale Antonio Gramsci, Piazza Beccaria and Piazza Piave, ending at the riverside. One may also choose to carry on from Piazza della Libertà, following Viale Don Minzoni and Viale dei Mille to **Campo di Marte**, with its sports installations, turning back toward town along Viale de Amicis and Via Piagentina to Lungarno del Tempio, Lungarno Giraldi and Piazza Piave.

Fiesole

Fiesole is Florence's Etruscan ancestor and an important Roman district town, strategically situated high on a hill above the Arno Valley. The access road which snakes up the hill offers wonderful views of the Arno Valley and of Florence. In the last century it was particularly popular with English tourists of all classes. Their florentine life and adventures have been documented and romanced in several novels, poems and films.

The simplest way to reach Fiesole is by *ATAF* bus Line 7, which leaves from the Florence's main bus terminal and carries on to its Fiesole terminal. There, on the main square, you'll also find the Fiesole *APT* information office (tel. 598.720).

Cross the main square (Piazza Mino da Fiesole), keeping the **Duomo** (better known as the Cattedrale di San Romolo) on your left. This Cathedral was built in the 11th century and subsequently amplied in the 13th and 14th centuries. Its **Belltower** dates from 1213. Within the Cathedral are several Della Robbia terracotta works and a number of paintings, frescos and carvings dating from the 14th and 15th century.

Follow the alley that runs behind the Cathedral to the Archeological Area, with ruins of a **Roman Theatre**, of **Baths** and of a **Temple.**

Fiesole has several interesting museums. The first you'll see on this itinerary, just across the alley from the entrance to the Archeological Area on your left, is **Museo Bandini** (open to visitors Wednesday-Monday, 10am-1pm and 3-6pm; tel. 59477), with a beautiful collection of early Renaissance Florentine paintings.

Turn right into Via Marini and then Via Portigiani until you come to two other important museums. On your left, at No. 9, is the **Antiquarium Costantini** (open to visitors Wednesday-Monday 10am-4pm, in the summer until 6pm; same tel, no. as the Bandini Museum), which exhibits the prestigious collection of ancient ceramics, donated to the town by Alfiero Costantini.

On your right is **Palazzina Mangani** at 24 Via Portigiani, seat of frequent modern art exhibitions (inquire at the Fiesole *APT* Office, tel. 598.720). An alley branches off Via Portigiani on your right; follow it to Piazza Garibaldi. Its northern side is fronted by several pleasant boutiques and cafés; follow it back to the eastern end of Piazza Mino da Fiesole.

Cross the length of Piazza Mino da Fiesole and climb Via di San Francesco, to visit two interesting late-medieval churches: **San Francesco** with its own Convent and Museum (tel. 59175; open daily 10-noon and 3-5pm); objects and documents are from ancient China and Egypt; in the church there are several important late Florentine Renaissance paintings) and **Sant'Alessandro**, a very ancient (4th century) church, built mostly with material looted from earlier Roman buildings.

On your way back to Florence, if it's not too late, you might stop briefly at the little **Borgo San Domenico** village with the church of the same name, which preserves several paintings by Beato Angelico. Not far from the church is the pre-Romanesque abbey **Badia Fiesolana** (restored in the 15th century).

The Medici Villas

The Medici rulers built seven great villas, where they, their families and their lovers, used to spend summer holidays. Some of the villas served them as love nests; others were used to take revenge on their enemies. All of them reflect the great riches of the Medici court.

All the villas are within easy reach of Florence, not farther than 30km. An organized day tour to those seven marvels might be available: inquire about this at the *APT* (tel. 230.2124), or at the *ATAF* information office (tel. 580.528).

POGGIO A CAIANO

This sumptuous summer residence was built for Lorenzo the Magnificent by Sangallo, with a vast garden and a majestic loggia, decorated with enamelled terracotta friezes.

The Ombrone River, which cut through the grounds, had formed a pleasant little island behind the villa. Lorenzo, who was also a poet of no little renown, named this island *Ambra* (Amber) in one of his poems; not soon after the Ombrone rose in anger and washed away Lorenzo's beloved little island.

A hall in Poggio a Caiano – Lorenzo the Magnificent's summer residence

The walls of the villa's great hall are covered with frescos by Andrea del Sarto, Pontormo and Allori. Here, during the summer of 1587, Francesco de' Medici fell suddenly ill and died in the arms of his beloved second wife, Bianca Cappello; only a few hours later Bianca also died – no one knows the cause; she was barely 40 years old.

The villa is situated 18 km west of Florence. Take *ATAF* line 35 or direct interurban *COPIT* bus from Florence's main bus terminal (near the railway station). Open daily 9am-6:30pm; entrance fee.

VILLA DI CAREGGI

This is where Cosimo the Elder and Lorenzo the Magnificent spent their last days. Lorenzo's doctor, accused of negligence, was summarily thrown into the courtyard well alive. The garden and the fortress-like front of the villa are worth a visit.

The Villa is situated 6 km north of Florence. Take *ATAF* line 14C from the main bus terminal; by car – follow the signs from the Prato highway. (Visit by appointment only; tel. 427.7329)

A grand chandelier in Villa di Castello

VILLA DI CERRETO GUIDI

This villa, built by Buontalenti for Cosimo I in 1565, is today the seat of a modest Medici Museum of portraits and furniture. It is the least interesting of the Medici Villas, in spite of its majestic front entrance.

Take a train to Empoli (30km) and then by *COPIT* bus to Cerreto Guidi. By car: follow the Florence-Leghorn Superstrada to the Empoli exit, and then follow the signs to Cerreto Guidi (7km north-west of Empoli). Open Monday-Saturday 9am-7pm, on Sunday and holidays 9am-2pm; entrance fee.

VILLA DI ARTIMINO

The villa was designed in 1594 by Buontalenti as a hunting lodge. From the garden, admire the 40 singularly shaped chimneypots aligned all along its roof. The view is splendid from the windows of its upper floor.

By car, follow the Florence-Pisa-Leghorn Superstrada for 12km to Lastra a Signa, and there follow the road signs to the Villa; by bus: *COPIT* to Poggio a Caiano and *CAP*

bus to Carmignano (by appointment only; tel. 879.2030).

VILLA DEMIDOFF

While the villa itself is little more than a ruin, its park preserves all its grandeur: a 30 hectare adventure-land with several well marked paths. The villa, built by Francesco I de' Medici for his beloved second wife, Bianca Cappello, was demolished after more than a century of neglect by Ferdinand III Lorraine. In 1872 the estate was sold to the Demidoff family, who undertook the restoration of the park and of some of the surviving original structures.

By car – travel 12km northward on the Bologna road to Pratolino, then follow the road signs to the Villa; by bus – *ATAF* line 25A from the Station. (Open only May-September, Thursday-Sunday 10am-8pm; entrance fee).

VILLA LA PETRAIA

The villa formerly belonged to the Brunelleschi family. Cardinal Ferdinand Medici, who acquired it in 1575, had it restored by Buontalenti. During the second half of the 19th century King Vittorio Emanuele II of Italy used it as his personal summer residence. The formal gardens and the unusual fountain *Florence Arising from the Waters* were designed by Tribolo.

By car – follow the Sesto Fiorentino road for 7km, and then follow the road signs to the Villa; ATAF bus 28. (Open daily 9am-7:30pm; joint entrance fee for this villa and Villa di Castello).

VILLA DI CASTELLO

This villa was used for centuries as a country cottage by the Medicis and the Lorraines, the archdukes of Tuscany. Today it serves as the seat of the *Accademia della Crusca,* a major documentation centre of the Italian language. In its attractive garden (originally by Tribolo) are several statues and monuments, the most famous of which is the statue of *Hercules and Antheus.*

The villa is in the vicinity of La Petraia, along the Sesto Fiorentino road *ATAF*: bus 28 (open daily 9am-7.30pm, winter until 6:30pm only, joint entrance fee for this villa and *La Petraia*).

The Renaissance style garden of Villa di Castello

AROUND FLORENCE

Some of the most beautiful towns in Italy are to be found at a distance of about an hour by car (or by rail) from Florence; along the route to those towns, there are also quite a few attractive and interesting sites to visit.

In this chapter we shall visit the fascinating towns of Tuscany along four main routes: to Siena, to Arezzo, to Pistoia and to Pisa.

Florence to Siena

Siena is situated 68km south of Florence, 322m above sea level in the heart of the famous Chianti hills (pronounced – *Kianti*). There is no direct railway connection between Siena and Florence but there is an excellent autostrada connecting the two.

The attractive Tuscan countryside

Leave Florence following the southbound Viale Petrarca to the point where it becomes Via Senese and then, at Tavernuzze, take the access road on the right to the autostrada. Should you miss it, don't worry: you'll find yourself on the narrower and longer old Roman **Via Cassia**, which stubbornly zigzags on to Siena; you'll be able to catch the autostrada at another point.

San Casciano in Val di Pesa is a pleasant place to stop. The Pesa is a tributary of the Arno, flowing from the higher Chianti hills to rejoin the Arno at Montelupo, not far from Empoli; this San Casciano is not to be confused with the perhaps better known health resort, almost 90km south of Siena.

San Casciano, a little town of 15,000 people, lies deep within the Chianti hills; the mountain sides are covered with the famous vineyards and peppered with lonely old farms. San Casciano grew in the Middle Ages around an ancient bishopric castle. In the course of the 14th century it became a walled city; the whole perimeter of the wall, with several bastions and four gates, is practically intact.

Cycling – a wonderful way of exploring Italy

The most interesting site in San Casciano is the Chiesa di Santa Maria del Prato, which has the richest art collection in the whole Chianti district.

Keep driving for the next 34km, to **Poggibonsi**. On the hillsides along the way you might catch a glimpse of the belltowers of some old monastery, abbey, or church. We would recommend stopping for a short visit at either Passignano (on your left) or San Lazzaro or Petrognano (on your right).

Passing through **Poggibonsi** (population 27,000), you'll probably notice that this little town is a junction of considerable importance, where major highways and minor roads converge on the way to Empoli, San Gimignano, Volterra, Siena and Arezzo.

The importance of this junction was recognized in antiquity; the Romans built here, up on the hill, the fortified bastion of *Podium Bontii* (hence the present name!). Today

Poggibonsi is a regional market town, with a few interesting medieval monuments, like the tall **Collegiata** tower and the **Chiesa di San Lorenzo**.

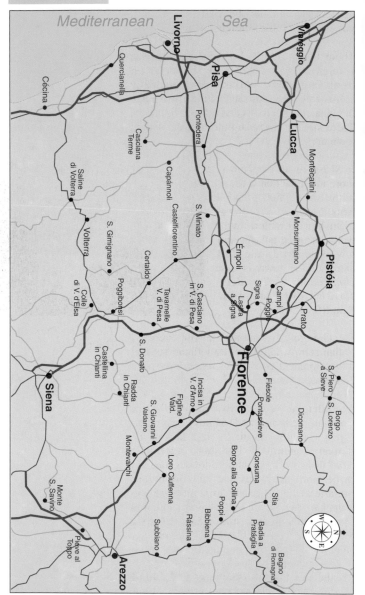

San Gimignano

This little town is an absolute must. It has to be seen to be believed. One might see all the marvels of the great Tuscan cities of Florence, Siena, Pisa, Arezzo and all the rest, but the true spirit of the unique region of Tuscany cannot be understood until you've visited San Gimignano.

There is no railway line that goes to San Gimignano. Approaching it by bus or by car from Poggibonsi (11km), one gradually seems to go back through time: first come the vines, olive groves and hillside orchards. Then, slightly higher up the hill, the walled town appears.

The towers of San Gimignano

In size, San Gimignano is more a village than a town, with only 7,500 inhabitants. Yet, it is a medieval township, complete with walls, fortified palaces and towers. Indeed, the full name of the town is *San Gimignano delle Belle Torri* (St. Giminian of the Beautiful Towers).

San Gimignano is an ancient town even by Italian standards. There are indications that it was founded by the Etruscans more than 25 centuries ago.

According to legend, two young Roman patricians, Silvius and Mutius, who had gotten in trouble during the last days of the Roman Republic, fled to those hills; they liked what they saw and built two fortified castles for themselves and their followers; centuries later Mutius' Castle became the *Mucchio* (today an old hamlet at San Gimignano's gates), and Silvius' Castle became the Forest's Castle (*Castello della Selva*).

Around the 11-12th centuries, minor local princes, harassed from time to time by their

Piazza della Cisterna, with the cistern in the middle

stronger neighbours in Florence or Siena, or by the Bishop of Volterra, got the idea to set themselves up with their own little walled town, within which they built for themselves and their people private fortified mansions, each equipped with its own tower.

For two centuries San Gimignano survived as an independent *comune*; then, in 1353, Florence took it over. In those days, the chroniclers claim that San Gimignano had no less than 72 private fortified towers. Today only 14 remain.

The town has remained practically unchanged for the last five centuries. It is, as we have already mentioned, very small, and can be traversed in a matter of two hours. Most of the town is closed to motor vehicles, and therefore it has to be visited on foot. Park your car in one of the parking lots near **Porta di San Giovanni** (St. John's Gate) (all of which are rather expensive!).

Enter the gate and follow Via San Giovanni, flanked by tourists' shops, restaurants and wineries. After passing the first three alleys on your left, climb toward the town's main square, the triangular **Piazza della Cisterna** (Cistern's Square), surrounded by more than half of San Giminiano's towers. The square owes its name to the beautiful medieval cistern, from which the citizens used to draw their drinking water. This is the heart of the little town.

Pass through the Cugnanesi Archway that leads into the square itself. On your left is the Town Hall or **Palazzo del Popolo** (People's Palace) with its tower, where in the year 1300 a young Ambassador of

Florence, Dante Alighieri, argued in favour of a Tuscan league in the Pope's defense (*La Lega Guelfa*). The Palazzo's halls are decorated with beautiful 14th century frescos; on the upper floor is the town's Pinacoteca, with a rich collection of 13th and 14th century works.

Across the street from the Town Hall is the old **Palazzo del Podestà**, with its two towers (one of them, the Torre Rognosa – or "mangy" – is the oldest tower in town).

Cross the square between the two above-mentioned palaces. The next square is Piazza del Duomo. The great church at the top of the wide flight of stairs is the **Duomo** (or Cathedral). Walk into the church; most of the rich frescos and paintings date to the 14th and 15th centuries. Don't miss *Santa Fina's Chapel*, a Renaissance masterwork by Benedetto di Maiano.

Across the square is the triple-towered **Palazzo Salvucci**. Follow the left wall of the Duomo, climbing toward the top of the hill where you'll find **La Rocca** (the Castle), with the most wonderful view of the town from its garden and walls.

Back on Piazza del Duomo, enter, on your left, Via San Matteo (more tourists' shops,

One of the towers surrounding the Piazza della Cisterna

leather shops and restaurants). On your right you'll see the **Chiesa di San Bartolo** and the **Palazzo Pesci-olini.** Follow San Matteo to the city wall, and turn right into Via Cellolese. At the end of this alley you'll see, on your left, the church of **Sant'-Agostino**.

Walk through these ancient alleys, with their old houses, and follow the walls toward the east until you come to **Chiesa di San Giacomo**. Behind the church is a minor gate, and there at the corner, on the outside, you will find a bus stop; any of the buses that stop here will take you back to St. John's Gate where you parked your car.

Back on the Siena Road, the next town to stop at is **Monteriggioni** (population 7,000), which is like an open air museum: its 13th century walls (only 570m in perimeter) and its 14 medieval towers have only been slightly "improved" over the last seven centuries, and they preserve all the flavour of their past.

From Monteriggioni, a 10km drive will bring you to Siena.

Siena

Siena (population 65,000) is a work of art in itself, in full harmony with its hills and its people. The secret of Siena's attraction is not the majesty of its churches and palaces or its squares and gardens; the whole city is magic.

Siena's area code is 0577.

APT Office, Piazza del Campo 56; tel. 280.551.

Hotel Information, tel. 288.084.

Coming from Florence, you will probably enter Siena through **Porta Camolla**, with its welcoming inscription *Cor Magis tibi Siena Pandit* ("Siena welcomes you with its great heart"). The walled city of Siena is closed to traffic; your car will have to be left at the outer parking, beside the gate.

Italy has always been a magnet for tourists

Proceeding from Porta Camollia, we come to **Piazza del Campo** – a Gothic jewel of unique beauty, one of the most beautiful squares

Night lights

in Italy. In this square is the **Palazzo Pubblico**, and **Torre del Mangia** (103m, 503 steps!). From the upper platform you'll have a breathtaking panoramic view of the town: behind the square is the Duomo and the Palazzo del Magnifico, to the south are the Palazzo Piccolomini and Palazzo Chigi-Saracini, to the east are San Martino and the Logge del Papa.

Just across Il Campo you'll find the *APT* office, on the ground floor of the Loggia della Mercanzia. Enter the building, the **Palazzo Pubblico**. This 13th-14th century palace is one of the most elegant buildings in Tuscany. The palace houses the **Museo Civico** (open to visitors daily 9:30am-7:30pm; closed on holiday afternoons; in winter 9-12:30pm; tel. 292263; entrance fee), and there is a real hoard of masterpieces: frescos (the great *Maestà* by Simone Martini), paintings and sculptures.

The square is shaped roughly like a sea shell, and its pavement is strikingly subdivided into nine sections, which converge at an apex situated at the entrance of Palazzo Pubblico, not far from a 15th century fountain, **Fonte Gaia** (by Jacopo della Quercia), a source of pride among the citizens of Siena.

Just under the tower is the **Cappella di Piazza**, completed in 1376.

A few steps east of the square is the **Palazzo Piccolomini**, an outstanding Renaissance palace housing the majestic **Biblioteca Piccolomini** archives (medieval documents, annals and illuminated manuscripts; it is open 10am-1pm and 2:30-5pm; tel. 280.626; entrance fee). Across the street is the vast **University Palace**.

Now walk back to Piazza del Campo, cross Via di Città and enter Via dei Pellegrini, which will lead you to the next great monumental complex: **Piazza del Duomo**, with Palazzo del Magnifico, the Duomo, Palazzo Arcivescovile, the Spedale di Santa Maria di Scala and the Prefettura.

Palazzo del Magnifico is a 16th century Renaissance palace built for Pandolfo Petrucci, a despotic ruler of Siena, self-named *Il Magnifico* (The Magnificent).

The **Duomo** has one of the most perfectly beautiful Tuscan Gothic façades, in white marble with pink and green inlays; its three majestic portals are richly decorated according to Giovanni Pisano's design. Above the central portal is an elaborated *rosone (*round crenellated window) by Giovanni di Cecco, and above the *rosone* is a perfectly preserved triangular mosaic.

The Duomo's belltower is primarily Romanesque, with six ranks of windows, starting with a single window at the lowest floor and ending with a sextet of windows on the highest floor. The whole tower is made of alternating black and white bands of marble.

The Duomo's floors are strikingly tiled in black and white, with a series of Biblical and New Testament motifs. The Duomo's upper floor houses a superb series of frescos by Pinturicchio. Don't miss the Cappella della Madonna del Voto, with its bronze and marble statues by Bernini. The Duomo Museum, **Museo dell'Opera Metropolitana** (open daily 9am-7:30pm in summer; in winter 9-12:30pm only; tel. 283.048) is a showcase of the Sienese Renaissance school of painting.

The Duomo also has an unusual history. Originally built in the early 12th century on the foundations of an older church, its end walls were razed to the ground two centuries later as part of an ambitious expansion project that would have extended the already vast church in the direction of the hillside. However, the enormous costs and the calamitous pestilence of 1348 blocked the works. The new additions were destroyed, and the Duomo finally achieved its present shape.

Behind the Duomo is the Baptistry, which would have originally been integrated within the grandiose super-church planned in the early 14th century. It is done in white marble, an unfinished masterpiece. In its interior are several important works of art.

The **Spedale di Santa Maria della Scala**, on the opposite side of the square, has a beautiful façade, rich of colourful Renaissance frescos.

Walk along the side of the great bulk of the **Prefettura**, following Via del Capitano until you come to the **Pinacoteca Nazionale**, (Via San Pietro 29; tel. 281.161; entrance fee). Housed within the **Palazzo Buonsignore**, this museum contains the most important collection of two centuries of Sienese painting, together with world famous painters of other schools.

Italian street signs point the way

Further on, you'll come to the church of **San Pietro e Paolo** (a trove of frescos and paintings) and **San Agostino** (a 13th century church restructured three centuries later by Vanvitelli).

Now walk back northward to Piazza del Campo along the winding Casato di Sopra and Casato di Sotto. Turn left and then right onto via di Città, an avenue of great private and public palaces; the name changes to Via Banchi di Sopra.

Having reached Piazza Salimbeni, stop at one of the three cafés before you carry on your walk to the neighbouring churches of Santa Maria di Provenzano, San Pietro Ovile and, at the end of Via dei Rossi, the vast and monumental San Francesco (15th century; frescos by Lorenzetti). All along the way you'll get a feeling for just how harmonious Siena is.

Up the Valdarno to Arezzo

The main road from Florence to Arezzo (84km) – the *Superstrada Aretina* (toll-free highway) – starts at Piazza Santa Croce in Florence, where it is known as Via Gioberti. It follows the course of the Arno river very closely, with minor deviations here and there, meandering through the Arno Valley, a dreamland of old farms, small villages and medieval ruins. It could rightly be called *castle and monastery country*.

After driving for 18km, past by several abbeys and castles, you reach the bustling market town of **Pontassieve** (population 20,000), seat of the main cellars of *Ruffino*, the major producers of Chianti regional vines. In May the annual *Toscanello d'Oro* wine festival is held in Pontassieve.

At Pontassieve take a left turn, eastward, to the Poppi-Bibbiena road to Arezzo. It is not much longer than the Aretina, nevertheless it is undoubtedly more interesting. The following brief comments will help you to make your choice of routes.

Along the Aretina Superstrada

Incisa (17km south of Pontassieve) is a small district market, where there are ruins of an old Florentine castle that include fragments of its perimeter, a gateway and the **Bandinella** observatory tower.

Figline (5km south of Incisa) is a little country town with the beautiful old medieval church of **Pieve di San Romolo**.

San Giovanni Valdarno, another 8km south-east, is a district town, built in the 13th and 14th centuries according to a design by the great Arnolfo di Cambio. Several charming old churches and palaces and a museum of Florentine Renaissance art are of interest to the tourist.

Montevarchi (located 5km south-east of San Giovanni) is a pleasant agricultural and industrial centre. In its church, **Collegiata di San Lorenzo**, there is a trove of sculptures and terracottas by the Della Robbia school. There is nothing much to see along the way from San Lorenzo to Arezzo (38km), except the beautiful countryside it-self.

Along the Bibbiena Road

From Pontassieve the road climbs to **Passo del Consumo** (1060m above sea level), at

Taking some time out along the way...

the southern border of the vast Parco Nazionale di Monte Falterona e delle Foreste Casentinesi. There are forests all around, and high mountains on both sides. The road first passes close to the old Castello di Romena, then even nearer the abbey of Pieve di Romena.

Poppi (population 6,000, 437m high), 35km east of Pontassieve, is a picturesque little town just below spectacular forests. The town is dwarfed by its majestic **Castello Pretorio** (13th-14th century) with its outside wooden staircase and corridors, which are quite well preserved. In its halls are valuable paintings, sculptures and frescos, mainly by the Della Robbia school. The local **Biblioteca Comunale Riliana** houses 20,000 volumes and more than 600 ancient *incunabula* (early 15th century printed works).

Bibbiena (population 11,000) is an ancient Etruscan town, with at least two interesting churches, and the Renaissance sanctuary of **Santa Maria del Santo** 1km east of town.

Bibbiena is 32km north of Arezzo. The road runs along the higher valley of the Arno, crossing several minor centres (Rassina, Calbenzano, Subbiano and Ponte alla

Chiassa) before descending gradually through the hillside from Bibbiena (425m above sea level) to Arezzo (296m above sea level).

Arezzo

Of Arezzo (population 95,000) it has been said that a walk through its streets represents a complete course in the history of Italian art. Indeed, it's very unusual to find, within an area of less than half a square kilometre, such relatively well preserved monuments and ruins representing three millennia of history.

Strategically situated at the junction of two great valleys – the Valdarno to Florence and Pisa and the Val di Chiana to Chiusi and southward to Rome – and surrounded by some of the most fertile farmland in Italy, it was settled very early by the Etruscans, who built it into one of their district capitals, and later by the Romans.

... and in the street

Among its sons are quite a few great names. The first is the legendary Maecenas (69-8 BC), whose name became a synonym of "patron" and "benefactor" of the arts.

Then there was Petrarch (Petrarca), the poet of the great *Dolce Stil Novo* (literally "Sweet New Style", the beginning of the new Italian language), who is rightly considered one of the founding fathers of the Italian language, along with Dante and Boccaccio.

A series of home grown

great Renaissance artists includes Spinello di Luca (the Aretino), Pietro Aretino, Vasari; Michelangelo Buonarroti was born in 1475 in Caprese, less than 45km away. In its heyday Arezzo was an independent medieval town and later (1384-1860) it became one of Florence's most prided possessions.

Arezzo's area code is 0575.

APT office: Piazza Risorgimento 116; tel. 23952.

THE SITES

The **railway station**, located near a parking lot and a bus terminal, is on Piazza della Repubblica, very close to the *APT* office, at the south-western edge of the old city. From the square, turn right on via Aretino and then left on via Margaritone. On your right, at the corner, you'll see the ruins of the **Roman Amphitheatre**; in the adjacent **Archaeological Museum** there is a rare collection of very ancient *coralline* pottery.

Via Margaritone ends at Piazza Sant'Agostino, with its church. Turn left onto Via Garibaldi, one of Arezzo's two major thoroughfares. Then turn right onto Corso Italia, the other main thoroughfare. The first church on your right is **San Michele**; the second is the **Pieve di Santa Maria** (12th century), one of the most splendid Romanesque monuments in Tuscany. Observe the majesty of its belltower. Next to it stands the magnificent **Palazzo della Loggia** by Vasari (16th century); across the square you'll see the 200m long Gothic-Renaissance façade of the **Palazzo della Fraternità dei Laici**.

Piazza Grande, behind the Pieve di Santa Maria, is the site of the internationally renowned monthly *Antiques' Fair* (first Sunday of each month) and of the September *Giostra del Saracino*, a unique medieval jousting contest held, of course, in full costume. On its north side are the **Logge del Vasari**; on its south side there is a series of very well preserved Gothic houses.

On the other side of Corso Italia is **Palazzo Pretorio** and next to it **Casa del Petrarca**, birthsite of the poet, today a museum in commemoration of his work. At the next corner, where Corso Italia ends and becomes Via Madonna Laura, turn right to stroll among the flowers and meadows of the spacious gardens of **Passeggio del Prato**. At the east end of the park is the pentagonal **Fortezza Medicea**, rebuilt in the 16th century upon the ruins of a medieval fort, and restored later again and again. From its bastions there is an excellent view of the town and the valley. At the north-western end of the Park is **Piazza della Libertà**, with the majestic mass of the **Duomo.** It was built in the 13th-14th centuries, but the Gothic façade was rebuilt at the beginning of the 20th century. Its wonderful windows are the work of the French glassmaster Guillaume de Marcillat. Next door to the Duomo, the **Museo Diocesano** has a rich collection of art works.

On the west side of Piazza della Libertà stands **Palazzo Bruni-Ciocchi**, an elegant Renaissance mansion with a striking inner courtyard. Enter via Sassoverde (northward) to Piazza Santo Domenico and the **Chiesa di San Domenico**, a splendid Gothic church from the early 14th century, with a very rich art treasure (a magnificent *Crucifix* by Cimabue above the main altar, and a series of 14th and 15th century frescos).

Turn left onto Via Santo Domenico and again left onto Via XX Settembre. Here is **Casa del Vasari**, the artist's birthsite and a museum. Where Via XX Settembre ends, at the corner of Via Garibaldi and Piaggia di Murello, is the most important **Galleria e Museo Medievale** (Medieval Gallery and Museum), with a rich collection of medieval art, as well as many works by Vasari and his pupils.

Follow Via Garibaldi southward and see the **Chiesa di Santissima Annunziata** (15th century); its stained glass windows are another example of the striking glasswork of Guillaume de Marcillat. At the next corner, turn left onto Piazza della Badia. The **Badia** is a 13th century church, expanded in the 16th century by Vasari. Its unusual belltower is from the 17th century.

Walk along Via Cavour eastward until you see on your right one of the most charming Umbrian-Tuscan Gothic **Basilica di San Francesco**, a single-nave Franciscan church built in the 14th century, with a 16th century belltower. Inside the church is Piero della Francesca's masterpiece fresco, the *Legend of the True Cross*.

From Florence to Prato and Pistoia

Pistoia is located 37km down the A11 Autostrada. The route itself is not spectacular, but more or less halfway along is Prato, a pleasant medieval town.

Prato

This is a busy market town (160,000 people), and one of Italy's major centres of the wool industry. But besides that, it is also a very ancient settlement, as witnessed by Etruscan ruins and fragments, by Roman monuments and by medieval palaces.

There is a convenient parking lot at the northern end of the Old City, on **Piazza Mercatale**. From Via Garibaldi turn right onto Via Verdi, toward the **Castello dell'Imperatore**, built in the 13th century in a severe nordic style for Emperor Frederick II of Hohenstaufen. When the emperor died the work was interrupted, never to be resumed. Nevertheless, the majestic structure and unfinished halls are used to this day for cultural events and art exhibitions.

Ancient Prato

On the castle square is the 15th century church of **Santa Maria delle Carceri** (by Sangallo). The other church, **San Francesco**, recognizable by its white and green stone walls, is a 13th century building, later improved by Sangallo. Walk on along via Rinaldesca to the **Palazzo Datini**, the great 14th century mansion of Marco Datini, a renowned banker, inventor of the *Letter of Exchange* (and of credit), Florence's main contribution to modern banking.

Prato's main square is **Piazza del Comune**, with the elegant **Fontana del Bacchino.** Along the square are the **Duomo** (Cattedrale di Santo Stefano), the **Palazzo Municipale** and the **Palazzo Pretorio.** The Latter is a 13th-14th centuries palace, housing important paintings and frescos in its Great Hall and in its Galleria.

The Duomo is a Romanesque-Gothic cathedral with a very interesting interior, a richly decorated choir and other spectacular elements; note its characteristic façade with its green and white bands. The **Museo dell'-Opera del Duomo** contains works by Carlo Dolci, the Lippis, Ghirlandaio, Paolo Uccello and others.

Pistoia

Pistoia's area code is 0573.

Pistoia (population 90,000) is a district capital and a regional market of garden and house plants and flowers. It's a medieval

walled town, built on the old Roman township of *Pistorium*. After two centuries of independence, it was engulfed by Florence until 1860, when all Florence's possessions became part of the new Kingdom of Italy.

The walled city is practically an open-air museum, centred around Piazza del Duomo (with an *APT* branch; tel. 21622). The **Duomo** (Cattedrale di San Zeno) has 5th century elements integrated into a 12th century beautiful Romanesque church. At the Duomo Museum there is a rich collection of silver and gold objects, illuminated manuscripts and other medieval documents of considerable interest.

Also on the Piazza are the **Belltower**, the **Baptistry**, the **Palazzo del Podestà** (Mayor's Mansion) and the **Palazzo del Comune** (Town Hall).

Ospedale del Ceppo (Hospital of the Alms) is a 13th century building superbly decorated with Renaissance stuccos and frescos.

South of Piazza del Duomo you'll see **San**

Giovanni Fuorcivitas (founded in the 8th century, rebuilt in the 13th in Pisan Romanesque style, with a trove of Renaissance paintings) and **Palazzo dei Bali** (14th-15th century; gracious inner courtyard). Also interesting are several other Pisan-Romanesque churches: **San Bartolomeo in Pantano** (1159), **San Pier Maggiore** (13th century), **San Domenico** (13th century) and the ancient church of **Tau** (10th century).

From Florence Westward: Empoli, Pisa and Lucca

Leave Florence westward, following the course of the Arno. We are on our way to one of Tuscany's major highlights, Pisa. Not far from Pisa there is another charming town, well-worth a short detour, Lucca. Unfortunately, the road that leads to them is far from attractive.

32km west from Florence you reach **Empoli**, a medieval country town of close to 50,000 people. First mentioned in several 8th century documents as "Empoli Castle", at the beginning of the 12th century it grew into an almost independent fief of the Guidi Counts, who in 1182 presented their town to the expanding Florentine Republic.

Today Empoli is a lively centre of industry and agriculture. The Old City is a little rectangle, centred around Piazza Farinata degli Uberti and enclosed within Via Chiara, Via Ridolfi, Via del Papa and Piazza Garibaldi.

Within this area there are at least four noteworthy structures. The **Collegiata di Sant'Andrea** church was rebuilt during the 11th century on the ruins of a very ancient chapel – one of the

The Camposanto in Pisa, which contains the tombs of many Pisan notables

earliest examples of the Florentine Romanesque style; the Church **Museum** contains scores of Renaissance works by famous Renaissance painters; the **Palazzo Pretorio** was, in Florentine days, the seat of the local administration; the **Palazzo Ghibellino** and its Paleontology Museum are also very interesting.

In Empoli there are also quite a few ancient little churches of interest: **St. Stephen** along Via dei Neri, the **Madonna del Pozzo** at the eastern end of Via del Papa and, on the eastern outskirts of town, at Pontorme, the unusually beautiful simple façade of **St. Martin**.

The SS67 *Superstrada* (toll free highway) carries on from Empoli westward through a series of little old hamlets to **Pontedera**, **Cascina** and Pisa.

Pisa

Pisa (population 110,000) is situated 82km west of Florence, and like Florence, it lies astride both sides of the Arno River. Pisa is a must, not only because of its leaning tower. Founded around the 6th century BC (probably by a seafaring tribe of Ligurians), it was first developed by the Etruscans and then by the Romans, who turned its natural harbour at the mouth of the Arno into a great military port.

After the fall of the Empire, Pisa continued to grow. Its fleets played an important role in stemming the Arab conquest. Then, in the 11th century, as an ally of Emperor Frederick the Redbeard, it was able to briefly annex all of Sardinia and Corsica, as well as the coasts of Tuscany. Its fleets ruled the Western Mediterranean until the end of the 14th century, when it was beaten definitively by Genoa and annexed by Medici Florence.

Under the Medicis it became a proud centre of study. The sea gradually retreated, and today, the city's only outlet to the sea, **Marina di Pisa**, is 11km west of the city centre. Pisa owes most of its great ancient monuments – the Duomo, the Campanile, the Battistero and the Camposanto Monumentale – to its own glorious school of architects.

Pisa's railway station is situated south of the River Arno, at the opposite end from the monumental centre, but Pisa is quite small and the spectacular Piazza del Duomo is only a 10m bus ride from the station.

The **Duomo** was built between the years 1064 and 1118 by Buscheto and Rainaldo. Together with the Battistero and the Campanile, the Duomo of Pisa is one of the most perfect showpieces of the Pisan Romanesque style, with its characteristic slender multiple floor colonnades. Beside the beauty of the structure itself, the interiors are of incomparable beauty; every small detail in the mosaics, stained glass windows, capitals, arches, sarcophagi, paintings and marble sculptured altars is a work of art.

The massive Duomo of Pisa

The marble **Battistero** is no less beautiful than the Duomo and perfectly harmonized with it, in spite of the fact that its design was drawn by another Pisan architect, Diotisalvi. It contains hundreds of sculptures, created by masters of the Pisan, Bolognese and Lombard schools.

The **Campanile**, or **Torre Pendente** – the world-famous Leaning Tower – was built toward the end of the 12th century by Bonanno. From the very beginning its foundations were unsteady, and construction works had to be interrupted after the third floor. One century later Giovanni di Simone added the next three floors, and the upper element was added toward the end of the 14th century. A 294 staircase climbs from the entrance to the upper terrace.

The Torre Pendente, Pisa's world-famous Leaning Tower

The fourth monumental element of Piazza del Duomo is the **Camposanto**, a rectangular structure built around the meadow growing on land brought by the Crusaders from the Calvary hill, in Jerusalem. It contains the tombs of many famous Pisan notables and a collection of Roman and medieval sculptures.

Also on Piazza del Duomo, along its southern side, are two museums: a **Museo dell'Opera del Duomo** and the interesting **Museo delle Sinopie**, with a unique collection of prime material used in the painting of medieval frescos.

Behind the first of these two museums is Piazza Arcivescovado, with the majestic **Palazzo Arcivescovile** (Archbishop's Palace). From this square, turn right into Via della Faggiola to Piazza dei Cavalieri, with its two churches and the towering **Palazzo dei Cavalieri** (Knights' Palace). Of particular interest is the larger of the two churches, **Santo Stefano dei Cavalieri**. All the buildings in this square are due to the great 16th century Vasari.

Follow Via San Frediano to the church, the University building and the riverside **Lungarno Pacinotti**. The long series of early Renaissance palaces that runs on both sides of the river is second in splendour and majesty only to Venice's Canal Grande. Short guided river cruises are available at the *APT*.

The wonderfully ornate marble Battistero in Pisa

North of the river there are several other interesting churches; worth mentioning are **San Caterina** (a 14th century Gothic style church) and **San Francesco** (with Taddeo Gaddi's 14th century frescos).

Pisa's area code is 050.

APT (very well equipped): 42 Lungarno Mediceo; tel. 522344.

Lucca

Lucca (population 90,000) is only 20km north-east of Pisa. Lucca's history is not unlike that of other Tuscan towns: it was

A medieval piazza in Lucca

first a Roman colony, then an independent city, seat of a local Duchy, gobbled up by the Bourbon French and eventually taken over by Florence.

But unlike elsewhere, its original medieval structure has remained practically intact within its 4,200m long reinforced walls (that have 12m high bastions and a 30m thick base. An outstanding promenade (highly recommended) runs on top of the walls today. All around the walls and their bastions is an inviting green belt, broken only by two sports fields.

Within the walls, the town is literally peppered with ancient churches, palaces and medieval towers. All the major sites can be seen and admired from the promenade on top of the walls.

Our walk starts at **Piazza del Risorgimento,** not far from the railway station, at the end of Via Regina Margherita. Having reached the promenade, you'll see, slightly ahead toward the East, the **Duomo** with its tall belltower. Built in the characteristic Pisan Romanesque style of the early 13th century, with its three ranks of pastel-coloured stone colonnades, the Duomo contains many medieval and Renaissance works of art.

An ornament at Santa Maria Forisportam

Across the square from the Duomo is another Romanesque church, **San Giovanni**. Walk along the promenade for about 300m, and you'll see on your left (within the walled city) another majestic Romanesque church, **Santa Maria Forisportam**. As you proceed along the **Giardino Botanico** (Botanical Garden) you'll see, on your right, the first two bastions: **San Colombano** and **Sant'Angelo**.

At the third bastion, **Cairoli**, the walls and the promenade turn northward. Pass above the **Porta Elisa** gate. Further on, at the top of the next bastion, **San Salvatore**, on your left is the **Museo Nazionale di Villa Guinigi**, which houses four centuries of sculptures and paintings from the late 14th century onward, as well as an interesting Etruscan collection. Nearby is the impressive 13th century façade of **San Francesco**.

The 13th century façade of the Chiesa di San Francesco

Abandon the promenade at this point and plunge into town. Follow Via dei Quarquonia to San Francesco, cross the square and carry on along Via dei Fratta. Enter via Mordini, and after two blocks you'll see on your left the ruins of the **Roman Amphitheatre**, which in the course of several centuries has gradually been transformed into a residential and trade complex; today it hosts, among others, the **market**.

Behind the amphitheatre is one of the most striking churches in Lucca, **San Frediano**, with a splendid tall Romanesque belltower and a mosaic façade. Like the Duomo, San Frediano was built in the 13th century upon the foundations of a 6th century church. Here, too, the interior shelters some very important works of art, among which Andrea della Robbia's *L'Annunciazione*.

At the corner of San Frediano, turn left on

Via Cesare Battisti with its little *trattorie*.
The street brings you to Piazza del Salvatore; cross it to reach **Chiesa di San Michele in Foro**, yet another outstanding example of the 13-14th century Pisan Romanesque style. Regrettably, this church, with its splendid four ranks of marble colonnades, has been rather negligently restored in recent years.

Across the square you'll see several majestic palaces. The southbound street, Via Vittorio Veneto, opens into Piazza Napoleone, whose western side is occupied by the vast façade of the 16th century **Palazzo di Provincia**; the majestic outer staircase dates from the 19th century.

Continue down Via Vittorio Veneto, cross the wide Corso Garibaldi and you'll end at Piazza Vittorio Emanuele, just where your walk began, on the outer side of the wall.

Lucca's area code is 0583.

APT: 2 Piazza Guidiccioni; tel. 491.205; also at Piazza Verdi; tel. 419.689.

MUSTS

For those short of time, below is a list of sites and sights to which Florence owes its fame, beauty and interest.

The Duomo complex: on Piazza del Duomo, the complex most representative of Florence's architecture, sculpture and painting; don't miss Giotto's Belltower, the Baptistry and Michelangelo's *Pietà* in the Museo dell'Opera del Duomo (see "The Heart of the Inner City", p. 48).

Chiesa di San Lorenzo: this church, with the **Cappelle Medicee**, is the second great complex of monumental art and architecture in the centre of medieval Florence; on Piazza San Lorenzo, only a stone's throw away from Piazza del Duomo (see "The Northern Inner City", p. 82).

Palazzo Vecchio: on Piazza della Signoria, an early 14th century castle-like, severe palace designed by the great Arnolfo di Cambio; once the seat of power of the Medicis, today it serves as the display case of hundreds of great art masterworks (see "The Medici Art Heritage", p. 64).

The Palazzo Vecchio and Piazza della Signoria

The Uffizi Gallery: deep within the hub of medieval Florence, its two floors contain the richest and most important collection of paintings and sculptures in Italy (see "The Medici Art Heritage", p. 67).

Palazzo del Bargello: this great fortress-

In the Gallery of the Academy – the famous "David" by Michelangelo

like medieval palace houses the **National Art Museum**, a complement to the major Florentine museums, on Via del Proconsolo (see "The Heart of the Inner City", p. 60).

Gallery of the Academy (Galleria dell'Accademia): an absolute must, if only to see the *Tribune of David*, the most famous statue of the Renaissance: the world famous **David** by Michelangelo (see "The Northern Inner City", p. 91).

Piazza della Santissima Annunziata: a beautiful harmonious square where you'll find the Chiesa della Santissima Annunziata and the Spedale degli Innocenti, as well as a splendid colonnade by Brunelleschi and a series of terracotta *putti* by Andrea della Robbia (see "The Northern Inner City", p. 91).

Palazzo Pitti: Florence's most imposing and largest Renaissance palace, housing no less than six museums and the magnificent **Boboli Gardens**, a fine example of a Renaissance-style garden that offers good views of the palace, the river and the whole city; on the Oltrarno southern side of the river (see "The Oltrarno and its Pearl", p. 97).

The Palazzo Vecchio

Ponte Vecchio: one of Florence's most famous landmarks; a bridge has stood here since Etruscan times. The triple archway bridge sports a double row of shops along its sides (see "From Ponte Vecchio to Santa Maria Novella", p. 69).

Chiesa di Santa Maria

Novella: many great Florentine styles are reflected in the architecture of this church, where they are integrated into a whole of great intrinsic harmony; on Piazza di Santa Maria Novella (see "From Ponte Vecchio to Santa Maria Novella", p. 78).

Chiesa di Santa Croce: the church is one of the greatest achievements of the Florentine Gothic architecture; a burial ground for Florence's famous sons, including Michelangelo, Galileo Galilei, Machiavelli and others (see "From Santa Croce to San Miniato al Monte", p. 104).

A wonderful example of the Florentine Gothic architecture – the Chiesa di Santa Croce

MAKING THE MOST OF YOUR STAY

Wining and Dining

Many Italians live under the preconception that Florentine cuisine is poor and basic because the simplicity of its terminology belies the artistic creativity of Florence's chefs.

Take, for instance, the famous *bistecca alla fiorentina* – a great chunk of barbecued beef for two hearty eaters (it may weigh as much as 1.5kg). To prepare it right, great artistry is required. First, the cut of meat is vital – beef sirloin from a grown and well exercised ox (never veal); the fire, ideally flaring embers of chestnut logs, is also important; salt, pepper and a measured sprinkling of olive oil must be added at exactly the right moment; and, finally, the barbecued beef has to be taken from the fire at just the right moment.

Perfection may be achieved in the simplest food. *Castagnaccio*, for instance, is nothing more than a simple chestnut-flour cake, which must be tried again and again to really appreciate it. Its perfect flavour, the absolute quality of its texture, its utmost lightness will probably manifest themselves to you at some simple neighbourhood bakery.

Florence, like most Italian cities, has its own secret pasta recipes, including *pappardelle al sugo di lepre* (home made pasta in hare sauce) and the very popular *pappa al pomodoro,* a tomato soup thick with rice and tomatoes.

The wines of Tuscany are excellent – the most famous is

be found at every second corner. It is common to drink coffee standing at the bar.

Here is a short glossary of coffee terminology to help you order:

un caffé – three minute sips of coffee cream to be sucked from tiny cups
ristretto – two sips of a thick, thick cream of coffee
macchiato – *caffé* "stained" with a drop of milk
cappuccino – the *caffé* is served in a slightly larger cup and topped with hot cream

the *Chianti*, but the *Sassicaia*, the *Brunello* and the *Tignanello* regional table wines are also deserving of appreciation.

Eateries in Italy go under different names:
Ristorante and **Trattoria** are practically one and the same – a restaurant.
Tavola Calda is a generaly cheaper and simpler establishment.
Tavola Fredda is a sandwich bar, with tables where cold cuts, wine or bear may be ordered.
Pizzeria needs no explanation.
Paninoteca is the stand-up, popular brand of the *tavola fredda*.

ESPRESSO
In Florence, like in most of Italy, coffee is not simply a drink but a ceremony. Most Florentines own at least one espresso machine, and a crowded bar or *caffé* can

A Gourmet's Basic Italian Glossary

ANTIPASTI – HORS D'OEUVRE
Anguilla Marinata – marinated eel
Bagna Cauda – hot anchovy and garlic dip
Funghi Marinati – marinated mushrooms

Melanzane Marinate – marinated aubergines
Caponata – aubergines in tomato sauce

ZUPPE, O MINESTRE, O PRIMI – SOUPS AND OTHER ENTRÉES
Zuppa di Cozze – mussel soup
Pasta e Fagioli – bean soup with pasta
Zuppa di Pesce – fish soup (many local variations)
Zuppa di Vongole – clam soup
Zuppa alla Pavese – chicken broth with poached eggs
Minestrone – vegetable soup
Stracciatella – chicken broth with flakes of eggs and cheese

PASTA, RISO E POLENTA – PASTA, RICE AND CORN-MEAL DISHES
Cannelloni – rolled pasta stuffed with meat and baked in tomato and cream (or other sauces)
Fettuccine – flat, long egg noodles
Gnocchi di patate – potato batter dumplings, boiled and served with various sauces
Gnocchi alla Romana – Gnocchi made of Semolina, baked with butter and cheese
Polenta – a boiled corn-meal pie of quasi-solid consistency
Risotto – rice cooked with various spices and meats or vegetables
Risi e Bisi – a particular Venetian risotto of rice and peas
Spaghetti alla Carbonara – spaghetti with bacon sauce and eggs
Tortellini – pasta stuffed with chicken and cheese (or other variations)

VERDURE – VEGETABLES
Fagioli all'Uccelletto – white beans with tomatoes and garlic
Finocchio al Forno – baked fennel
Broccoli alla Romana – broccoli braised with white wine
Cavoli in Agrodolce – cabbage in sweet and sour sauce
Piselli al Prosciutto – peas with cured ham
Pomodori alla Siciliana – baked tomatoes stuffed with anchovies, tuna fish and black olives
Peperonata – braised sweet peppers with tomatoes and onions
Sformato di Spinaci – spinach soufflé
Carciofi al Tegame alla Romana – baked stuffed artichokes
Zucchini Ripieni – stuffed courgettes baked in tomato sauce
Peperoni Imbottiti – baked stuffed peppers

INSALATE – SALADS
Insalata Mista – tossed green salad
Insalata di Pomodori – tomato salad
Fagioli Toscanelli con Tonno – bean and tuna-fish salad
Insalata di Riso – rice with cold meat, vegetables and more

PESCE – SEAFOOD
Aragosta – lobster
Ostriche – oysters
Fritto misto – mixed fried fish
Grigliata mista – mixed grilled fish
Scampi – prawns
Trote – trout
Calamaretti fritti – fried inkfish

POLLAME – POULTRY
Anitra Arrosto – roast duck
Pollo con Peperoni – chicken braised with tomatoes and peppers
Tacchino Arrosto Ripieno – roast stuffed turkey

CARNE – MEAT
Bistecca alla Fiorentina – grilled rib steak (generally for two)
Cervella fritta – fried veal brain
Lingua – tongue
Maiale – pork
Osei scampai – literally, "birds that fled", a spicy dish of thin veal, cheese and ham parcels braised in a tomato and red wine sauce
Osso Buco – braised veal shanks
Prosciutto – ham in various forms
Scaloppine di vitello – veal escalopes in assorted sauces
Trippa – tripe
Testina di vitello – boiled veal cheeks

DOLCI – DESSERTS
Gelati – ice-cream
Granite – sorbet (flavoured water ices)
Cenci alla Fiorentina – fried pastry twists
Pere Ripiene – pears stuffed with gorgonzola cheese
Panettone – fruited yeast cake
Pesche Ripiene – baked peaches stuffed with macaroons
Crostata di Ricotta – Roman cheesecake
Zabaione – sugared egg pudding with marsala wine
Spuma Gelata di Marsala – frozen zabaione
Cassata alla Siciliana – Sicilian cake with chocolate icing
Dolce Torinese – chilled chocolate loaf

Restaurants

THE BEST
Enoteca Pinchiorri: 87 Via Ghibellina, tel. 242.777; closed on Saturdays, all August and the Christmas season. Housed in the modernized interiors of a great Renaissance palace; classic and regional cuisine, and superb wines. Very expensive.

Relais le Jardin: 5 Piazza d'Azeglio, tel. 245.247; closed on Sundays. Elegant, superlative classic cuisine; situated within the *Regency Hotel*. Very expensive.

Sabatini: 9a Via dei Panzani, tel. 282.802. An old, traditional establishment; international cuisine tempered by surprisingly genuine local specialties. Expensive.

EXPENSIVE

Dino: 15r Via Ghibellina, tel. 241.452. Closed on Sunday nights, on Mondays and from August 1-20. The chef has a very personal touch; highly recommended.

Cantinetta Antinori: 3 Piazza Antinori, tel. 292.234. In the 15th century Antinori Palace, serves regional dishes in an atmosphere of friendly elegance.

Il Cibreo: 118r Via dei Macci, tel. 234.1100; closed on Sundays, Mondays, August 27 to September 5 and for the Christmas season. One of the most authentic traditional regional cuisines.

RELATIVELY INEXPENSIVE

Antico Fattore: 1 Via Lambertesca, tel. 238.1215; closed on Sundays, Mondays, August 4-20 and the Christmas season. Traditional cuisine, very central (near the Uffizi Gallery).

Del Fagioli: 47r Corso Tintori, tel. 244.285. Closed on Saturdays, Sundays and all August. Traditional regional cuisine.

Trattoria da Guido: 34r Via Faenza, tel. 289.746. Closed on Wednesdays. Very central, modest but tasty, fixed price lunches.

Trattoria da Cesarino: 16r Via G. B. Niccolini, tel. 247.9169. Closed on Sundays. A very good family restaurant, with several unique specialties at very convenient prices, recommended.

MOSTLY FISH

I Quattro Amici: 29 Via degli Orti Oricellari, tel. 215.413.

Vittoria: 52 Via della Fonderia, tel. 225.657.

PIZZA

Casa del Vin Santo: 15/17r Via Porta Rossa, tel. 216.995; open till late at night.

La Greppia: 4/8 Lungarno Ferrucci, tel. 681.2341.

Il Grande Nuti: 22/24 Via Borgo San Lorenzo, tel. 210.145.

Palazzo Pitti, the Museo dell'-Opera del Duomo and others. For detailed seasonal programmes, ask at the *APT* Office.

There are several cinemas and small theatre halls; the weekly programmes are available at the reception desk of most hotels as well as at the *APT*s.

CHINESE
Il Mandarino: 17 Via Condotta, tel. 239.6130.

Nanchino: 40r Via de' Cerchi, tel. 213.142.

PIANO BARS AND DISCOTEQUES
Caffé Tornabuoni: a piano bar, 12-14r Lungarno Corsini, tel. 210.751.

Central Park: piano bar and disco, 1 Parco delle Cascine, tel. 333.488.

Full-up: disco, 21 Via della Vigna Vecchia, tel. 293.006.

Culture and Entertainment

Florence's night life is moderate and cultured; during the world famous *Maggio Fiorentino* musical season (operas, concerts, recitals and theatre) it becomes rather hectic and crowded.

Off season, there are frequent evening spectacles, happenings and concerts at several of Florence's main museums including the Palazzo Vecchio, the Stibbert Museum, the Medicis' Chapels, the Horne Foundation, St. Mark, the Istituto degli Innocenti, the

Il Barretto: piano bar and grill, 50 Via del Parione, tel. 294.122.

Maracanà Discoteca: disco and Brasilian spectacles, very central, 4 Via Faenza, tel. 210.298.

Ottorino Club: a piano bar, 6r Via Elisabetta, tel. 284.579.

Rockafé: piano bar and disco, 66 Borgo Albizi, tel. 244.662.

Villa Kasar: disco, piano bar and restaurant, 23 Lungarno Colombo, tel. 676.912.

Yab: disco, 5 Via Sassetti, tel. 282.018.

Several hotels also have an in-house piano bar:

Anglo-American Hotel Regina: 9 Via Garibaldi, tel. 282.114.

Excelsior Italie: 3 Piazza Ognissanti, tel. 264.201.

Grand Hotel: 1 Piazza Ognissanti, tel. 288.781.

Majestic: 1 Via del Melarancio, tel. 264.021.

Plaza Lucchesi: 38 Lungarno della Zecca Vecchia, tel. 26236.

Savoy: 7 Piazza della Repubblica, tel. 283.313.

Villa Medici: 42 Via Il Prato, tel. 238.1331.

Where to Shop and for What

Florentine speciality shops sell leather, footwear, artistic pots, jewels, silks, antiquities, books, wines and liquors – some of them at the best international standards, other at unique Florentine standards.

LEATHER

Albert di Barbieri Roberto: 22r Via Guicciardini, tel. 282.846.

Christian: 36r Via della Scala, tel. 280.674.

Gazzarrini Giuseppe: 71r Via Porta Rossa, tel. 212.747.

Gori G.: 64r Via Faenza, tel. 282.174.

Leoncini Firenze: 13r Via Ginori, tel. 210.008.

Mannelli Pelletterie: 56r Ponte Vecchio, tel. 219.325.

Maria's Leather Goods: 13r Via Finiguerra, tel. 238.2740.

Pelletterie Gioberti: 58r Via Gioberti, tel. 669.555.

FASHION

Gianfranco Ferré: ladies' and gentlemen's boutique, 52r Via dei Tosinghi, tel. 292.003.

Giorgio Armani Boutique: high fashion for ladies and gentlemen, 51r Via della Vigna Nuova, tel. 219.041.

Lacoste: 33r Via Vigna Nuova, tel. 316.693.

Paolo Tonali: ladies' fashion, 7r Via Roma, tel. 213.583.

Trench: young fashion wear, 2 outlets: 10r Borgo San Lorenzo, tel. 280.014 and 16r Via Porta Rossa, tel. 287.601.

BP Studio: knitwear, 2 outlets: 24r Via Vacchereccia, tel. 239.8955; 15r Via della Vigna Nuova, tel. 213.243.

Laurel: 67-69r Via della Vigna Nuova, tel. 284.922.

Mariposa: ladies' high fashion, 2 Lungarno Corsini, tel. 239.8985.

FOOTWEAR

Calzature Fiorenza: 41r Rione Borgo S. Lorenzo, tel. 239.6025.

Calzaturificio Fratelli Rossetti: 43r Piazza Repubblica, tel. 216.656.

Casadei: 33r Via Tornabuoni, tel. 287.240.

Gilardini-Calzature Magli: 8r Via Cerretani, tel. 212.412.

Romano: 13r Borgo S. Lorenzo, tel. 284.725.

ARTISTIC POTTERY

Galleria Machiavelli: 39r Via Por Santa Maria, tel. 239.8586.

JEWELS

Argenteria Tozzi: 19 Ponte Vecchio, tel. 283.507.

Cardini di Lamperi: 34r Ponte Vecchio, tel. 212.928.

Cassetti: 52/54r Ponte Vecchio, tel. 287.361.

Fratelli Piccini: 21/23r Ponte Vecchio, tel. 294.768.

Romano Gioielleria: 35/39 Via Cerretani, tel. 211.048.

Barducci Bardo & Son: 22 Via Strozzi, tel. 230.2322.

Giuliano: 41r Via Guicciardini, tel. 292.106.

ANTIQUITIES

Ars Antiquaria: 3 Lungarno Soderini, tel. 294.626.

Zecchi Antichità: 34r Via Maggio, tel. 293.368.

Galleria Bellini Luigi: 5 Lungarno Soderini, tel. 214.031.

Campolmi: 5 Via Maggio, tel. 295.367.

SILK

Antico Setificio Fiorentino: 4 Via Bartolini, tel. 213.861.

BOOKS

BM Bookshop English Books: 4r Borgo Ognissanti, tel. 294.575.

Paperback Exchange M.: 31r Via Fiesolana, tel. 247.8154.

Vallecchi Editore SPA, 21 Via
il Prato, tel. 290.765.

CAMERAS AND FILMS
Bongi: 80/84 Via Por S. Maria,
tel. 239.8811.

Foto Ottica Spina: 1r Via
Battisti, tel. 211.113.

Studio Immagine SDF: 202r
Via Ghibellina, tel. 288.667.

WINES AND LIQUORS
Chianti Ruffino SPA: 8 Via Por
S. Maria, tel. 210.771.

Consorzio Vino Chianti: 4
Lungarno Corsini, tel. 212.333.

Enoteca Bonatti: 66r Via
Gioberti, tel. 660.050.

Il Cantinone: 5r Via S. Spirito,
tel. 218.898.

Street Markets
Mercato delle Pulci (Flea

Market): Piazza de' Ciompi;
daily except July. Ancient furniture and art objects, coins,
jewels, prints etc.

Sant'Ambrogio: Piazza
Ghiberti; weekday mornings
only. Food, fruits, vegetables,
flowers, footwear and clothing.

Mercato di San Lorenzo: on
the beautiful Piazza San
Lorenzo; closed on Sundays
and Mondays. Clothing, leather
and souvenirs.

Important Addresses and Phone Numbers

EMERGENCIES
Carabinieri (emergencies): tel. 112.
Police (emergencies): tel. 113.
Fire Brigade: tel. 115.
Medical Emergencies: tel. 118.
ACI – Road Assistance: tel. 116.
City Police: tel. 36911; emergencies, tel. 352.141.
Railway Police: tel. 212.296.
Cardiac Emergencies: tel. 214.444.
First Aid: tel. 212.222.
Hospital Information: tel. 27591.
Night Medical Service: tel. 477.891.

ALL NIGHT GAS STATIONS
Agip – Via Rocca Tebalda

Agip – Via A. del Pollaiuolo
Esso – Viale Europa
IP – Viale Giannotti
Mobil – Via Pratese
Q8 – Viale Pratese (Sesto Fiorentino)
Tamoil – Via Senese
Texaco – Viale Guidoni

AIRLINES
Alitalia: 10-12r Lungarno degli Acciaiuoli, tel. 27888.
British Airways: 36r Via Vigna Nuova, tel. 218.665.
KLM: 2 Piazza Antinori, tel. 284.043.
Lufthansa: 6 Via Pellicceria, tel. 238.1444.
Olympic: 4 Via Por S. Maria, tel. 282.338.
SAS: 8 Lungarno Acciaiuoli, tel. 238.2701.
Swissair: 1 Via Parione, tel. 295.055.
TWA: 4 Via dei Vecchietti, tel. 239.6856.
Sabena: 1 Via Tornabuoni, tel. 211.001.

CONSULATES
Austria: Via dei Servi, tel. 238.2014
Belgium: 28 Via dei Servi, tel. 282.094
Denmark: 13 Via dei Servi, tel. 211.007
Finland: 6 Via Strozzi, tel. 293.228
Germany: 30 Lungarno Vespucci, tel. 294.722
Great Britain: 2 Lungarno Corsini, tel. 284.133

Norway: 26 Via G. Capponi, tel. 247.9321

Spain: 21 Via La Pira, tel. 217.110

Sweden: 4 Via della Scala, tel. 239.6865

Switzerland: 5 Piazzale Galileo, tel. 222.434.

USA: 38 Lungarno Vespucci, tel. 239.8276

MISCELLANEOUS

Road Conditions Information: Rome, tel. 06.4212.

Urban Transportation

Information: Piazza Stazione, tel. 580.528.

Railway Information: tel. 288.785.

Lost and Found: Via Circondaria 19, tel. 367.943.

Railway Station Luggage Service: tel. 212.319.

Porters Coop.: tel. 212.319.

Radio Taxi: tel. 4242, 4798.

Customs: tel. 214.316.

Post Office: Via Pietrapiana 53-5, tel. 217.941; information; tel. 160.

Telephone Booking Office: tel. 214.145; information, tel. 184.

Dictionary

PRONUNCIATION KEY

a	*"a"*	as in *"car"*
e	*"e"*	as in *"set"*
i	*"ee"*	as in *"eel"*
o	*"o"*	as in *"over"*
u	*"oo"*	as in *"soon"*
ci	*"chee"*	as in *"cheese"*
ce	*"che"*	as in *"chess"*
chi	*"kee"*	as in *"key"*
che	*"ke"*	as in *"kettle"*
gi	*"jee"*	as in *"jeep"*
gi + vowel	*"j"*	as in *"Julia"*
ge	*"je"*	as in *"jelly"*
gh (before e and i)	*"g"*	as in *"go"*
gl (before e and i)	*"lli"*	as in *"stallion"*
gn	*"ni"*	as in *"onion"*
s between two vowels	*"z"*	as in *"rose"*
sc (before e and i)	*"sh"*	as in *"shore"*

ENGLISH	ITALIAN
good morning	*buon giorno*
hello, goodbye	*ciao, addio*
good evening	*buona sera*
good night	*buona notte*
please	*per favore*
thank you	*grazie*
pardon, excuse	*scusi*
yes	*sì*
no	*no*
what...?	*che cosa...?*
when...?	*quando...?*
where...?	*dove...?*
there is...	*cè...*
there is not...	*non cè...*
what is the time?	*che ore sono?*
how are you?	*come sta?*
far	*lontano*
near	*vicino*
big, large	*grande, grosso*
small	*piccolo, piccino*

ENGLISH	ITALIAN
new	*nuovo*
old	*vecchio*
right	*destra*
left	*sinistra*
first	*primo*
last	*ultimo*
open	*aperto*
closed	*chiuso*
entrance	*entrata*
exit	*uscita*
car	*automobile*
bus	*autobus*
bus station	*fermata dell'autobus*
train	*treno*
railway station	*stazione ferroviaria*
subway, underground	*metro*
ticket	*biglietto*
taxi	*taxi, tassi*
plane	*aereo*
airport	*aeroporto*
boat, ship	*barca, nave*
port, quay, wharf	*porto, mollo*
slow	*lento*
fast	*veloce*
gas	*benzina*
gas station	*stazione di rifornimento*
hotel	*albergo*
hostel	*pensione*
room	*camera*
toilets	*servizi, bagno*
bath, shower	*bagno, doccia*
restaurant	*ristorante*
café	*caffé*
table	*tavola*
chair	*seggiola, sedia*
waiter	*camariere*
water	*acqua*
bread	*pane*
drink	*bevanda*
menu	*menù*
hot	*caldo*

DICTIONARY

ENGLISH	ITALIAN
cold	*caldo*
soup	*freddo*
meat	*zuppa*
salad	*carne*
bill	*insalata*
receipt	*contoricevuta*
shop, store	*bottega, negozio*
pharmacy	*farmacia*
newsstand	*chiosco*
post office	*ufficio postale*
hospital	*ospedale*
police	*polizia*
embassy	*ambasciata*
market, bazaar	*mercato*
how much does it cost?	*quanto costa?*
expensive	*caro*
cheap	*a buon mercato*
cinema	*cinema*
theatre	*teatro*
road, highway	*strada*
street	*via*
avenue	*viale*
square	*piazza*
alley	*vicolo*
esplanade	*passaggio*
bridge	*ponte*
monument	*monumento*
fountain	*fontana*
church	*chiesa*
palace	*palazzo*
fort, castle	*castello*
town, city	*città*
village	*villaggio*
museum	*museo*
park	*giardino pubblico*
east	*est*
north	*nord*
west	*ovest*
south	*sud*
valley	*valle*
mountain	*monte, montagna*

ENGLISH	ITALIAN
range	*catena*
hill	*collina*
forest	*bosco*
river	*fiume*
Sunday	*Domenica*
Monday	*Lunedì*
Tuesday	*Martedì*
Wednesday	*Mercoledì*
Thursday	*Giovedì*
Friday	*Venerdì*
Saturday	*Sabato*
January	*Gennaio*
February	*Febbraio*
March	*Marzo*
April	*Aprile*
May	*Maggio*
June	*Giugno*
July	*Luglio*
August	*Agosto*
September	*Settembre*
October	*Ottobre*
November	*Novembre*
December	*Dicembre*
1	*uno, una*
2	*due*
3	*tre*
4	*quattro*
5	*cinque*
6	*sei*
7	*sette*
8	*otto*
9	*nove*
10	*dieci*
11	*undici*
12	*dodici*
13	*tredici*
14	*quattordici*
15	*quindici*
16	*sedici*
17	*diciassete*
18	*diciotto*

DICTIONARY

ENGLISH	ITALIAN
19	*diciannove*
20	*venti*
21	*ventuno*
30	*trenta*
31	*trentuno*
40	*quaranta*
50	*cinquanta*
60	*sessanta*
70	*settanta*
80	*ottanta*
90	*novanta*
100	*cento*
101	*centouno*
110	*centodieci*
120	*centoventi*
200	*duecento*
300	*trecento*
400	*quattrocento*
500	*cinquecento*
600	*seicento*
700	*settecento*
800	*ottocento*
900	*novecento*
1000	*mille*
2000	*duemila*
million	*un milione*

Index

INDEX

INDEX

NOTES

NOTES

QUESTIONNAIRE

In our efforts to keep up with the pace and pulse of Florence, we kindly ask your cooperation in sharing with us any information which you may have as well as your comments. We would greatly appreciate your completing and returning of the following questionnaire. Feel free to add additional pages.

Our many thanks!

To: Inbal Travel Information (1983) Ltd.
18 Hayetzira St.
Ramat Gan 52521
Israel

Name:

Address:

Occupation:

Date of visit:

Purpose of trip (vacation, business, etc.):

Comments/Information:

INBAL Travel Information Ltd.
P.O.B 1870 Ramat Gan
ISRAEL 52117